Contemporary Architect's Concept Series 4
Studies by the Office of Ryue Nishizawa

Contemporary Architect's Concept Series 4

Ryue Nishizawa: Studies by the Office of Ryue Nishizawa

Seventh published in Japan on March 1, 2025 by TWO VIRGINS.

TWO VIRGINS
4-1-3 Kudankita, Chiyoda-Ku, Tokyo 102-0073, Japan
TEL: +81 03 5212 7442   FAX: +81 03 5212 7889   https://www.twovirgins.jp/

Authors: Ryue Nishizawa, Ippei Takahashi

Publisher: Chiyuki Sumitomo

Editing and Planning: Media Design Research Ltd.

Translation: Thomas Daniell, Haruki Makio / Fraze Craze Inc.

Cover Design: Satoshi Machiguchi

Print: Yamada Photo Process Co., Ltd.

© 2009 by Office of Ryue Nishizawa

All rights reserved. No part of this book may be reproduced or utilized in any form or by any information
storage or retrieval system, without prior permission in writing from the copyright holders.

Printed in Japan   ISBN978-4-86791-043-6 C0052

西沢立衛 ｜ 西沢立衛建築設計事務所スタディ集

目次

作品

ニューヨークのヴィラ　　　　　　　　10
ニューヨーク州、アメリカ／住宅／2008-

ガーデンアンドハウス　　　　　　　24
東京／住宅兼オフィス／2006-

森山邸　　　　　　　　　　　　　　36
東京／住宅／2002-2005

十和田市現代美術館　　　　　　　　44
青森／美術館／2005-2008

House A　　　　　　　　　　　　48
日本／住宅／2004-2006

モントリオールの展覧会　　　　　　58
モントリオール、カナダ／展覧会／2008

エモナホテル　　　　　　　　　　　60
エモナ、ブルガリア／ホテル／2006-

小山登美夫ギャラリー代官山　　　　74
東京／ギャラリー／2007

永井画廊　　　　　　　　　　　　　76
東京／ギャラリー／2008

熊本駅東口駅前広場　　　　　　　　78
熊本／駅前広場／2007-

軽井沢研究所　　　　　　　　　　　84
長野／研修所・展示館／2007-

t-project　　　　　　　　　　　　94
香川／美術館／2004-

本プロジェクト　　　　　　　　　104
2008-2009

エッセイ

スタディについて　　　　　　　　　6
西沢立衛

ランドスケープな建物　　　　　　34
髙橋一平

都市と氷山　　　　　　　　　　　42
髙橋一平

Index

Works

Villa in New York 10
New York, USA / Residence / 2008-

Garden & House 24
Tokyo, Japan / Residence + Office / 2006-

Moriyama House 36
Tokyo, Japan / Residence / 2002-2005

Towada Art Center 44
Aomori, Japan / Museum / 2005-2008

House A 48
Japan / Residence / 2004-2006

CCA exhibition 58
Montreal, Canada / Exhibition / 2008

Emona Hotel 60
Emona, Bulgaria / Hotel / 2006-

TKG Daikanyama 74
Tokyo, Japan / Gallery / 2007

Nagai Garou 76
Tokyo, Japan / Gallery / 2008

Kumamoto Terminal 78
Kumamoto, Japan / Terminal / 2007-

k-project 84
Nagano, Japan / Gallery / 2007-

t-project 94
Kagawa, Japan / Museum / 2004-

Book Project 104
2008-2009

Essay

On Studies 8
Ryue Nishizawa

A Landscape Like Building 35
Ippei Takahashi

City and Iceberg 42
Ippei Takahashi

スタディについて
西沢立衛

　昔からスタディというものが、僕はけっこう好きである。完成された建築物ももちろん好きだが、スタディというものに昔からなぜか惹かれつづけている。また、それによって出てきた図面やラフ模型、スケッチなどのスタディの残骸も、完成物とは違ったものとしての得がたい魅力があって、好きだ。建築物というものは完成されていて、静的で、動くことがないが、スタディというものはつねに未完成で、流動的である。そこには建築創造の瞬間を捉えたかのようなダイナミズムがある。

　もちろん、スタディが好きだといっても、やっていてつらいときもある。つらいときのほうが多いと言ったほうがいいかもしれない。いい案がどうやっても出ない状態というのがあって、それはかなり苦しい期間である。それが長引くこともあるし、出口がぜんぜんないときも多々ある。しかし、にもかかわらず、というかそうだからこそ、スタディというものに僕は、ある特別な魅力を感じている。スタディに向かうということは、なにか巨大な岩石に張り付くような苦しさ、つらさがあり、かつ同時に、ある充実感というのか、なんともいえないある種の快楽的な部分があるような気がするのである。スタディがつらいんだったらやらなければいいじゃないかと人は思うかもしれないが、気付くと僕はスタディに向かっている。たぶん僕は建築的・空間的な難題に取り組み試行錯誤することが好きで、その難問が解けるか解けないかとは別に、そういう難題と格闘して、へとへとになること自体に、なにかジョイみたいなものを感じているのだと思う。第一、スタディというものがもしもまったく快楽でないなら、もしそれが苦痛と義務、労苦だけだったら、僕は学生時代からいまにいたるまで20年以上にわたってスタディし続けていない気がする。朝起きて事務所に行ってうんうん考え苦しんで、ふと気付くと日が暮れていて、自分が長時間にわたってスタディに没頭していることに気付く。それは不思議な、疲労感と充実感をともなう体験である。みんなで打ち合わせしていて、先が見えないまま暗礁に乗り上げたり、もしくは、家への帰り道でどういう納まりがいいか考えたり、そういうことのすべてが僕にとってはたぶん、創造することの快楽なのだ。要するにスタディというのは、おもしろい。それは何度やっても、もう二度とやるもんかとはけっして思わない。スタディには、こうしないといけないというルールがないという点も、僕は好きだ。どんなアプローチもOKである。コンピュータを使ってもいいし、模型からやってもいい。ルールは特になくて、あえていえば「すごい建築をめざす」というそれだけが唯一の原則で、それ以外はどんな方法でやっても構わない。スタディというのは、建築を創造したいと願う人間だけが体験することができる、たいへん大きな自由なのである。

そういうふうに考え進めてきた結果、今回のこの本では、完成された建築の姿をフィーチャーするのではなく、思い切ってスタディということそれ自身をテーマにできないか、と思うようになった。なので、完成された建築の姿がほとんど出てこないものとなった。その代わり、いろんなスタディ案が出てくる。現実の建築物として実現されたスタディ案と、近い将来実現されるであろうスタディ案と、設計過程で残念ながら破棄されたスタディ案とを、どれも等しく載せることにした。また、あまりに遠い過去のプロジェクトは外した。そうすることで、自分たちが近年リアルに感じているテーマ、もしくは悪戦苦闘していること、スタディをとおした僕らの最近の関心事、そういうことをおぼろげながら描けるのではないかと考えた。ここで掲載したスタディ図版は、手描きスケッチ、コンピュータの落書き、CAD、打ち合わせ時の走り書きメモ、模型コラージュ、フォトコラージュ、ダイアグラム、etc.である。それらおのおのの魅力、素材の内容をなるべくそのまま感じられるように、色や素材感、順番や並び方などを工夫して掲載した。かつおのおのに簡単な解説を加えて、どういうスタディをやっているのか読み取れるページ構成を目指した。ページ数が限られているために、全スタディは掲載できず、僕らが事務所内で現実に行なっているスタディの実態、悪戦苦闘のすべてをお伝えすることはできなかったが、そのかけらみたいなことだけでもここで表わせないかと思った。

　今回スタディ集をつくるにあたって、過去の自分たちの建築プロジェクトのスタディの束をあらためて振り返ってみた。いろいろなものが出てきて、スタディというのは開放的なものなんだなあとあらためて思った。姿形はつねにあやふやで、どっち方面にだって育っていけそうな未知の雰囲気が一枚一枚に感じられる。スタディする側にしても僕だけでなく、いろんなスタッフの試行錯誤が、一緒くたに混ざっている。要するに誰でもいいというと語弊があるが、スタディというのは誰でもやろうと思えばできる、非常に開放的な場なのである。すごい案を思いつくかどうかという難問の前では、熟練の建築家も一年目の所員もまったく対等で、膨大な費用と労力をかけた精密なCGを、5秒くらいで描かれた落書き一枚が創造的に乗り越えてしまうこともある。スタディというものは、どんなに小さなスケッチ一枚にも、新しい建築の可能性に向かおうとする姿勢みたいなものがある。形のないものに形が与えられてゆくまさにその瞬間瞬間の連続がスタディであり、それは建築が生まれ出てくる現在進行形の創造そのものなのである。そういった、スタディという創造行為が持つ素晴らしさと可能性を、この本を手にとってくださった読者の皆さんが、僕らのつたないスタディの山積みをとおしてなんとなくでも感じていただければ、僕としてはこれに勝る喜びはない。

On Studies

Ryue Nishizawa

For a long time now, I have quite liked studies. I also like completed buildings, of course, but for some reason I have long been attracted to studies. Moreover, I also like the debris that results from making studies - drawings, rough models, sketches, and so on - as they have an elusive charm that differs from that of completed objects. Buildings are complete, static, motionless, but studies are always incomplete, fluid. Therein lies a dynamism, as if capturing the moment of architectural creation.

Of course, having said that I like studies, there are times when making them is arduous. You could probably say that it's arduous most of the time. There are situations where, no matter what you do, good ideas just won't appear, and those are quite painful periods. They can drag on, and often there seems to be absolutely no exit. Yet nevertheless, it is precisely for this reason that studies hold a special charm for me. Making studies is arduous and painful, like clinging to a large rock, yet at the same time I somehow feel a sense of fulfillment, and in part a kind of indescribable hedonism. Though there might be people who think that if studies are so arduous then just don't make them, but I have noticed that I gravitate toward studies. Maybe I like the trial and error of tackling difficult architectural and spatial challenges, but leaving aside whether or not these difficult problems can be solved, grappling with those challenges leaves my body exhausted and I feel a kind of joy. In the first place, if studies were completely without pleasure - if they were only agony, obligation, exhaustion - I doubt that I would have kept making them for more than twenty years, from my school days until now. Getting up in the morning, going to the office, grunting to myself in painful deliberation, suddenly noticing that night is falling, I realize that I spend long periods of time absorbed in making studies. These experiences provide a mysterious sensation of exhaustion as well as satisfaction. Have meetings with everyone, running into obstacles and not knowing how things will turn out, or else thinking about how to fit things together while on the way home, for me all of this is, perhaps, the pleasure of creating. In short, studies are interesting. No matter how often I make them, I have never thought to myself that I won't do it again. I like the fact that there are no rules on how studies should be made. Any approach is okay. You can use a computer, you may start with a model. Without specific particular rules, with the sole principle being to audaciously say, "I'm aiming at great architecture"; aside from that, any method at all fine. Studies provide huge freedoms, and experiences only available people with the desire to create architecture.

As a result of continuing to think along these lines, I began to feel that in this book, rather than featuring images of completed buildings, I would make studies my theme. So, there are hardly any images of completed buildings.

Instead, there are various study proposals. Included on an equal footing are study proposals that have been implemented as actual buildings, study proposals that will be implemented in the near future, and study proposals that unfortunately were abandoned during the design process. Moreover, projects from the distant past have been omitted. In doing so, I thought that through studies I might be able to faintly depict our recent concerns, the themes that we have felt were of real importance over the last few years, or our fierce struggles. The illustrations of studies published here include hand-drawn sketches, doodles on the computer, CAD drawings, memos scribbled during meetings, model collages, photo collages, diagrams, and so on. To give the maximum sense of their raw charm and material content, this publication has been devised to show their colors and materiality, their sequences and the ways they were aligned. A brief explanation of the kind of study being done has been added each one, with the aim of creating legible page compositions. Because the number of pages is limited, all the studies could not be published, so the full extent of the studies that we have been actually doing in our office and all of our fierce struggles could not be conveyed, but I thought that they might be represented here by just these fragments.

In making this collection of studies, I once again looked through a stack of studies from our past architectural projects. All kinds of things appeared, and I was reminded of how expansive studies are. The vague shapes on each sheet give a sense of the atmosphere of not knowing in which direction they will be developed. Scattered throughout the studies are a medley of experiments by various staff members, not only me. My point is, though it would be misleading to say that anyone can do it, studies provide a very expansive place to which anyone can contribute if they decide to try. Before addressing the difficult issue of whether or not a great idea can be hit upon, a single scribble drawn in about five seconds might creatively outstrip precise computer graphics that require huge cost and labor, giving complete equality between a skilled architect and an employee who has been in the office for less than a year. However small the sketch, a study takes the stance of trying to approach new architectural possibilities. In giving shape to something shapeless, studies undeniably have a continuity from moment to moment, and it is this present-progressive form of creation itself from which architecture arises. Nothing would give me greater pleasure than if, through this pile of our clumsy studies, every reader holding this book in their hand can somehow gain a sense of the wonders and possibilities contained in the creative act of making studies.

translated by Thomas Daniell

ニューヨークのヴィラ
Villa in New York, 2008-

ニューヨーク州で現在設計している、小さな住宅である。マンハッタンから車で3時間、大自然の山の頂に建つ。山頂なので360度ぐるりと遠望でき、眺めが素晴らしいので、地上から切り離された「空中に浮かぶヴィラ」を考えた。柔らかくカーブした有機的な形が、木々を避けながら、空中を漂うように浮かぶというものだ。

This is a small villa that I am presently designing. It is built on the crest of a mountain, a three-hour drive from Manhattan. With the extraordinary panoramic view from the mountain top, we imagined this "villa floating in air," separated from the ground. The villa takes an organic form with gentle curves wafting through the trees.

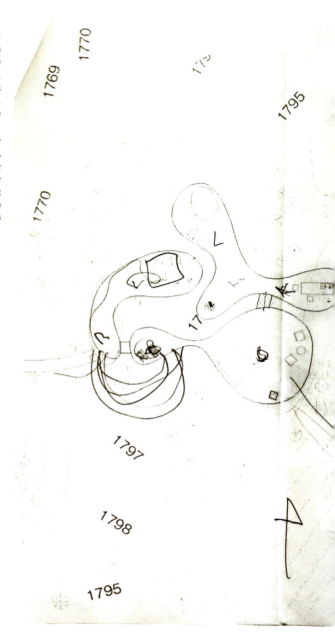

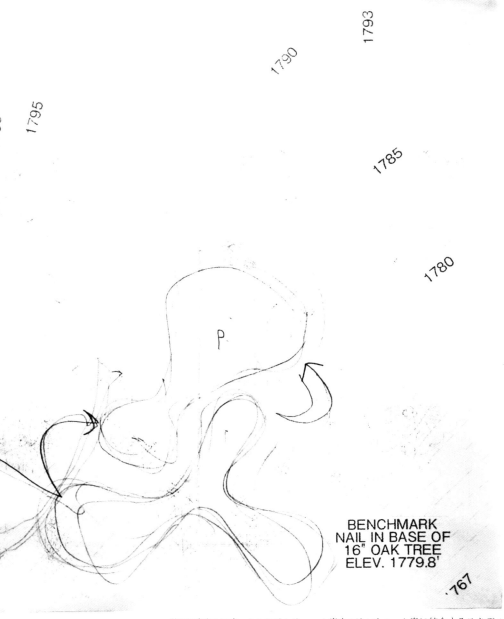

第240案と241案。3つのヴォリューム案を2ヴォリューム案に統合するスタディ
Plan No.240 and No.241. A study integrating three volumes into two

ニューヨークのヴィラ Villa in New York 11

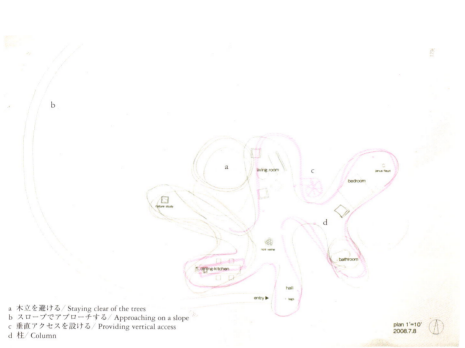

a 木立を避ける / Staying clear of the trees
b スロープでアプローチする / Approaching on a slope
c 垂直アクセスを設ける / Providing vertical access
d 柱 / Column

第275案。2ヴォリュームをさらに1ヴォリュームへ合体してみる
Plan No.275. Two volumes to be integrated into a single volume

カーブしながら木々を避けつつ、宙に浮かぶ単一形状の案、その立面
The plan and elevation of a single form which curves avoiding the trees, while appearing to float in the air

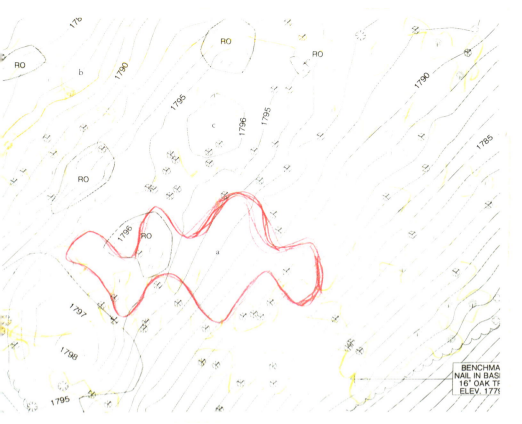

第309案。奥行きが浅く、木々と混ざりやすい横長形へと形を変えた案
Plan No.309. The plan for a thin form which blends easily with trees

a 住宅／House
b スロープ／Slope
c 林／Forest

ヴォリュームをひとつにまとめ、形をスタディする。奥行きの小さい横長に伸びる形によって、林の環境がより近づいて感じられるようになる。
The volume is integrated into one form. The thin, elongated form brings the forest closer.

ニューヨークのヴィラ Villa in New York 13

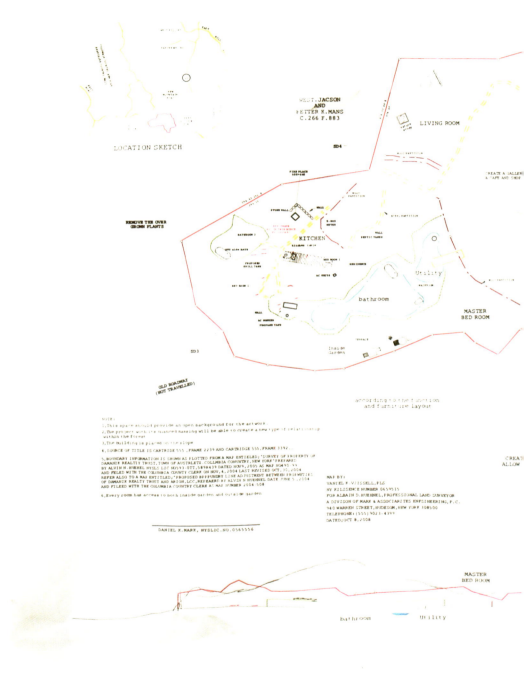

第188案の平面図。本敷地図を縮小して建築にしてみた案。地図のような平面と起伏が生まれる
Floor plan for Plan No.188. This option has a plan like a map which follows the undulations of the site

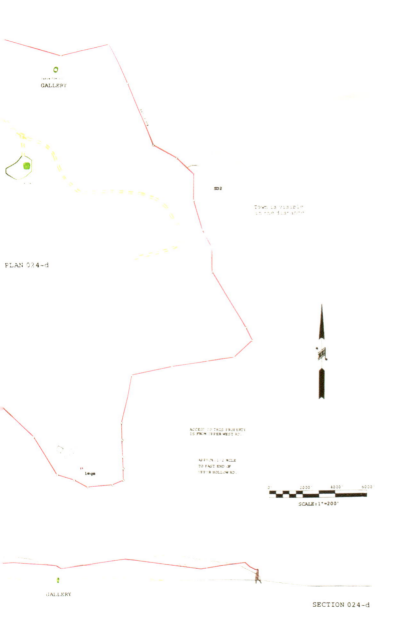

ニューヨークのヴィラ / Villa in New York

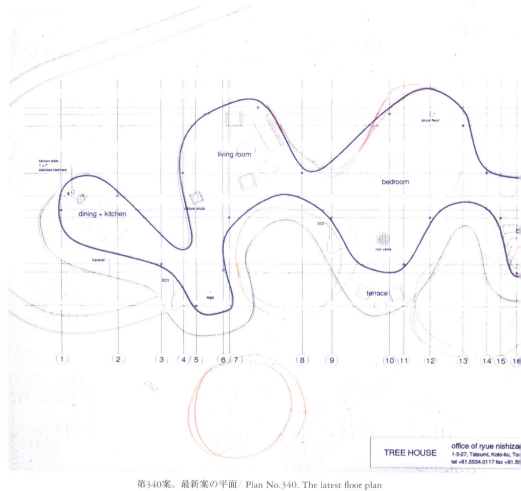

第340案。最新案の平面/ Plan No.340. The latest floor plan

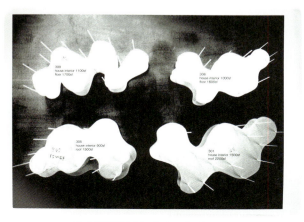

サイズの検討/ Analysing the size

大自然に囲まれた樹上の生活 / A life amidst the trees, surrounded by nature

最新案は、全部が空中に浮いた、ツリーハウスとなった。環境エンジニアとのやりとりから形が最適なものに変わっていった。太陽高度の低い冬は南面から光と熱を採り入れるため、南立面を東西に長くし、夏の強い日射しをカットするため南に庇を設けた。空調は地熱を利用し、エネルギー消費を抑える。庇の下にテラスを付けて、木々の中に飛び出す樹上の生活を楽しむことができるようになった。

The form has been optimized, in collaboration with an environmental engineer. In order to provide light and heat from the south in the winter time, the south facade has been made longer. An eave has been added across the south facing section. On the terrace set under the eave, the client can float among the trees.

第47案の配置図。林を四角く切り取り、その環境がそのまま住宅となる

Plan No.47. A square is cut into the forest, where the dwelling is to be built

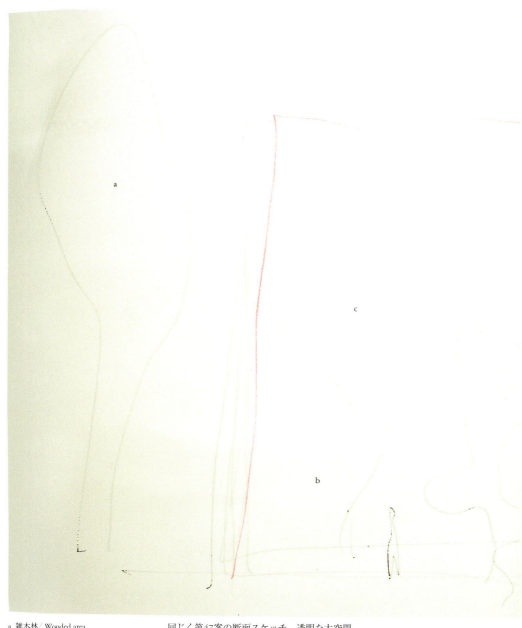

a 雑木林 / Wooded area
b リビング / Living room
c 部屋ごしの樹木 / Trees over the room
d バスルーム / Bathroom
e 巨大な天窓 / Huge skylight

同じく第47案の断面スケッチ。透明な大空間
Section sketch of No.47

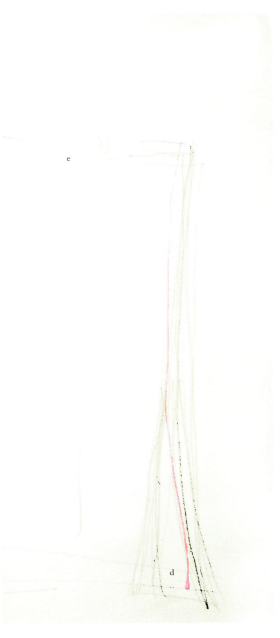

模型 / Model

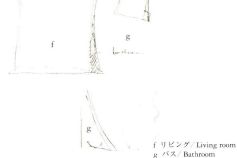

f リビング / Living room
g バス / Bathroom

平面スケッチ / Floor plan sketch

樹木と同じくらいの高さを持つ平屋の四角い部屋。アクリルでつくられた巨大で透明なヴォリューム。インテリアが林をのみ込み、外からは存在がわからないほど林に溶け込むヴィラ。
A one-storey square room which is as tall as the trees. A huge and transparent volume. The design allows the villa to swallow the forest, allowing it to fit into the forest, as though invisible when seen from the outside.

ニューヨークのヴィラ / Villa in New York

第216案。家具とアート作品が並ぶ。外は360度展望できる / Plan No.216. Furniture and art arranged on the site

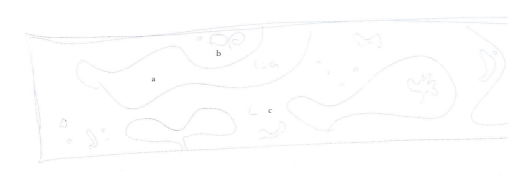

同、平面スケッチ。カーブした光庭がいろいろな部屋をつくりだす / Plan sketch. An undulating garden creates rooms

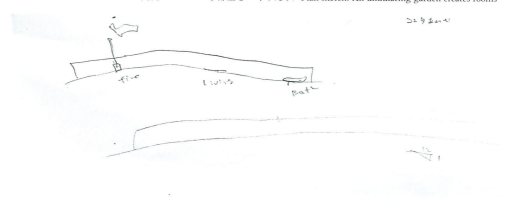

同、断面。床と屋根は平行なスロープとなっている / Section. The floor and roof have parallel slopes

第216案は、山頂の地形に寄り添って、だらっと広がった低い平屋の住宅。屋根勾配は敷地傾斜面と同一形状の3D曲面で、屋根と床が平行のまま上がったり下がったりする。室内の中央に山頂があり、空間を分けている。

Plan No.216 is a one-storey dwelling extending transversely to fit the landscape. The roof has 3-D curves similar in form to the inclined surface of the site. The roof and the floor rise and fall in parallel. The mountain peak at the center divides the interior space.

a 中庭／Courtyard
b 外の林／Forest Outside
c アートコレクション／Artworks

a 中庭／Courtyard
b アートコレクション／Artworks
c リビング／Living room
d 寝室／Bedroom

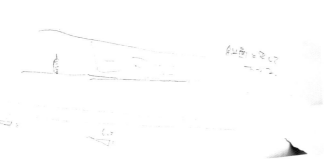

ニューヨークのヴィラ Villa in New York

ガーデンアンドハウス
Garden & House, 2006-

4 設計全般に関する要望

4-1 方向性

●柔軟性ではなく可塑性のある家

これは、物事全般に対する私の考え方というほうが正しいかも知れませんが、それが建物にも反映されるとよいと思っています。

その多くは、フランスの哲学者カトリーヌ・マラブーの著書『私たちの脳をどうするか』（春秋社　2005年刊）に依拠しています。この本は、ネオテロサイエンスが発達した時代（現代）における哲学的思考をどうするかというテーマを扱っています。

これによれば、柔軟性というのは、いわゆる状況適応能力をいい、それに対して、可塑性はもっとポジティブに変わっていくこと、つまり環境変化に適応するというよりも、もっと過激な変化です。たとえば、状況によっては破壊的なまでの爆発を行なって、思い切り新たなかたちを創造する力、進化する力をいいます。

生き方的に言えば、現状におもねることなく、つねに破壊と創造を繰り返し続ける勇気をもつ、といったところでしょうか。

これを、家に適用するならば、どうなるのか、ちょっとわかりませんが、まあ、安易にどうにでも使い道を変えることができるような形態や間取りの家ではないということはいえます。

従来の家造りに囚われることなく、この場所、この施主としか成立しえない、オリジナルの、創造性に満ちた、どこにもない、革新的な、しかし、どこにでも広がっていくことのできる本質的な家、ということになるでしょうか。

●来るべき住空間を目指す

考えてみますと、従来の住居とは家族がひとつの単位でした。家族構成の一般的なパターンは夫婦2人、夫婦2人と子1〜3人、2世帯（夫婦とその子ども夫婦とその子）5〜7人。いずれも血縁でつながる家族です。しかしながら、21世紀は戸籍上の家族ではない構成が増えると考えます。たとえば友達同士、知り合い同士など。さまざまな動機から共同生活をはじめる人々が増えていくと思われます。かくいう私どもも、このタイプの住人です。こうした人々の住居が新形態として定着していきそうです。

そのような家を未来の住居と呼ぶことにします。これは従来の枠組みとは何が違ってくるか、考えてみました。まず、夫婦の寝室や子ども部屋というものはなくなります。変わりに住む人の数だけ個室があるということになるでしょう。おおまかにいうと、個室と共同スペースの2つの組み合わせからなる住空間です。高齢化社会に突入する未来の日本においては、なおさら、この形態が今後の主流になると思います。

来るべき住空間は、住まう人間が血縁関係ではなく、なおかつ住人構成はつねに変化する可能性をはらんでいる住空間ということになります。
そのような住居の理想形について、ひとつの答となるよう家でありたいと願っています。

クライアントからの設計要望書
The design request from the client

●LOHAS の家

最近よく耳にする言葉ですが、LOHASとは、Lifestyles Of Health And Sustainability の略語で、健康的なライフスタイルと持続可能な環境を目指すという意味です。生活においては自然のリズムに逆らわない、オーガニックなスローライフのことです。住まいにもこのことを当てはめることはできないかどうか。シックハウスを避ける。無駄なエネルギーを使わない（省エネルギー）、石油エネルギーに頼らない、空気を汚染しない、環境付加の少ない素材を使う、といったことを意識していきたいと思います。

4-2 意匠について

●全体について

とくにこれといった要望はありませんが、原則として建物のボリュームは、4階建て・地下無し・延床面積が100平米くらいを希望します。西沢さんのデザインは大胆にして繊細で美しく、機知に富んでいますよね。そのような西沢さんらしさが発揮されることを望みます。

加えて、周辺環境だけでなく、この地域一帯の目来的な都市像を見据えたときにあるべき姿であったらと願います。つまり、今の環境に合わせるのではなく、この建物や街の未来が変わっていくような、この街の未来を映すような建物であることを望みます。

●屋根について

勾配屋根は雨漏りしやすく、メンテナンスにコストがかかるためNGです。屋上緑化がランニングコスト高からないのであれば、興味があります。

●ファサードについて

空調、換気、不審者等からの防犯面を兼備し、屋内が見えにならないような工夫をお願いします。

●エントランスについて

入り口はオフィス用とプライベート用の2つがあるとベストです。プライベート用は、非常口、勝手口の機能も兼ねたものがよいです。

— 6 —

---

① 個室 2室

② アーカイブ 1室

a. 書籍・資料収納庫

b. コピー・プリンタ置き場＋アシスタントデスク

③ ギャラリー兼ミーティングルーム 1室

●グレー・ゾーン

グレー・ゾーンとは、プライベートでありオフィシャルである空間のことです。

●食べる・集う・体験する 1室

全11ページの一部
A part of the 11 page-long request

• A house with plasticity, not flexibility

This is probably my way of thinking about things in general, but I hope it will be reflected onto my building as well. This concept significantly relies upon the book "What Should We Do with Our Brain?" (Perspectives in Continental Philosophy) authored by Catherine Malabou (published by Shunjyu publishing in 2005). The book takes up the theme of dealing with philosophic thought at the present time, when neuroscience has been developed. According to the book, flexibility is the ability to adapt to a situation well, while plasticity is the ability to change positively and drastically, rather than just simply adapting to environmental changes. It is the ability to create something totally new, in the manner of an explosion, which could be destructive depending on the situation, or in other words, the ability to evolve.

Likening this idea to a way of life, it would be to always have the courage to continue the process of destruction and creation, without compromising to the present situation.

I'm not really sure what'll happen if this concept is applied to a house, but it is true that the house I am talking about is different from one whose form and layout can be easily and freely changed depending on it intended usage. It would be a unique, creative, progressive and fundamental house, which could not be found anywhere in particular but could spread out to reach everywhere, and could only be built on that particular site and with that particular client, without being tied to the tenets of conventional housing construction.

• For future living space

The conventional housing unit in Japan has been a single family household. The typical patterns for this family structure are a couple (2 people), a couple and one to three children (3 to 5 people), or two households (an elderly couple and one of their married children and their children, 5 to 7 people). In each of these cases the individuals are relatives. However, I can imagine a proliferation of patterns in the 21st century, the majority of which are not based on a family register, but on other groups of people, such as a like-minded friends or acquaintances. More and more people will begin to cohabitate from variety of different motives. I and my housemates are actually now this type of resident. The dwellings for such cohabiters can be assumed to be established as a new form.

ガーデンアンドハウス Garden & House

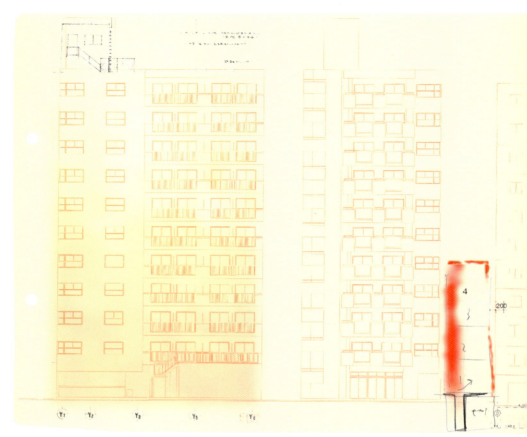

ビルとビルに挟まれた谷底のような極小の敷地に建つ。仕事仲間二人がここで共同生活をし、仕事もする、住宅のようなオフィスのような寮のような建物である

It is built on the smallest of sites, as if at the bottom of a valley, sandwiched between buildings. This is a building which can serve as house and office, where two colleagues can live and work together

敷地／Site　　　　　　　　　　　ビルに挟まれている／Sandwiched

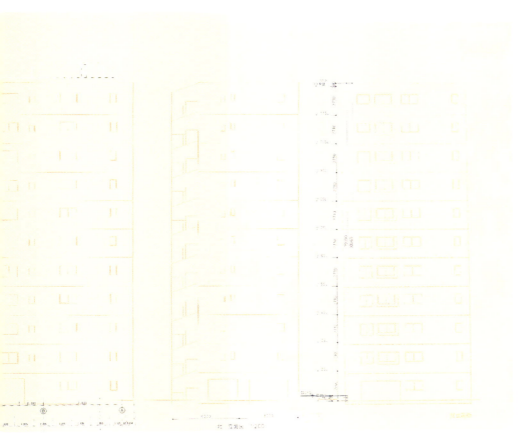

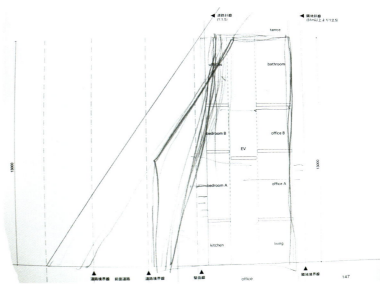

高さ制限に応じて曲げる / Sliced in accordance with city code

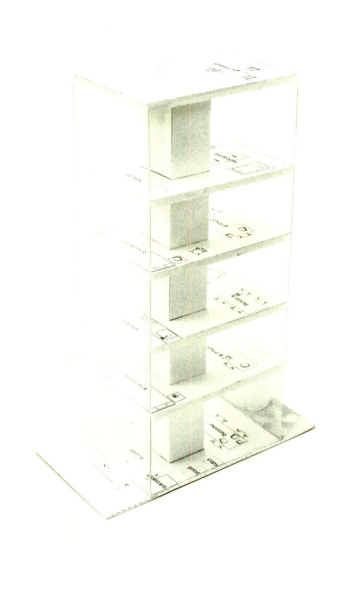

垂直に立つタワー案/ Plans of the vertical tower

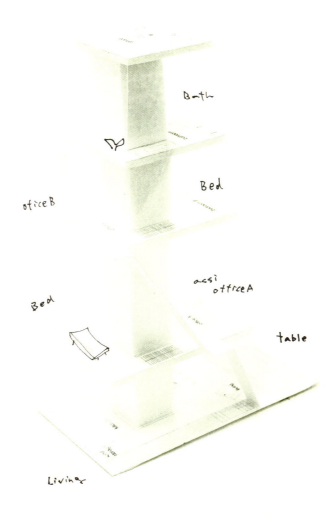

末広がり案。外階段が建物の周りを回る / Plans of the flared tower

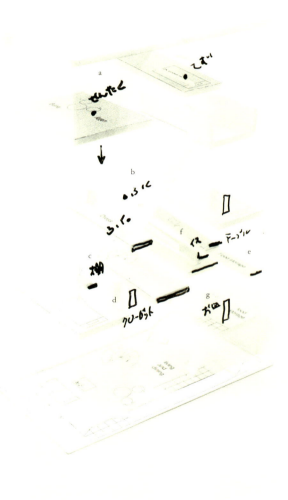

a Laundry
b Clothes
c Shelf
d Closet
e Table
f Chair
g Pantry

スキップフロア案／Plans of split-level tower

テラスが空中に浮かぶ案 / Plans of the terraces floating in the air

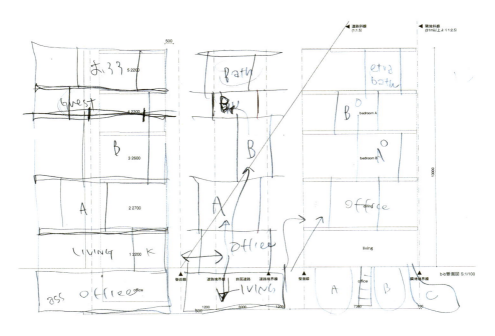

断面のスタディ
Study of a section

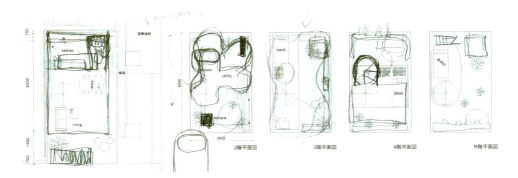

平面のスタディ。部屋の形は用途に合わせ自由に計画できる
Study of the floor plan. The form of the room can be flexibly designed according to its intended use

最新案にもっとも近い案。すべての部屋が庭を持ち、積層されてゆく。いろんな場所で読書したり夕涼みをしたり、開放的に東京都心の生活を楽しむことができる。
All the rooms have their own gardens. The floors layered together. Reading a book or cooling off in the evening in the various places of the building, they can enjoy their urban life in Tokyo openly with gardens all around.

庭と部屋のセットが積み重なる／Piling up sets of gardens and rooms

ガーデンアンドハウス Garden & House

ランドスケープな建物

髙橋一平／西沢立衛建築設計事務所

東京都内に計画した「森山邸」について。森山邸は、昔ながらの庶民的な住宅街に建つ。人も建物も開放的で、道での立ち話や近所の物音が平気で聞こえてくる。森山さんは、この街で酒屋を営んでいた。森山さんからの設計依頼は、酒屋を建て替え、自宅に加え、友人の家と数部屋のアパートをひとつの敷地に建てることだった。

スタディのはじめのうちは、この3種類の住宅をひとつの建物にまとめていた。それは、どっしりとした、ただのつまらない建物に見えた。そればかりか、まわりのどの家よりも巨大で、不特定多数が出入りする中身のわからない閉鎖的な建物を彷彿とさせた。要するに、開放的なこの街にあわない気がした。そこで、すべての住宅を一戸建てにする案をつくってみた。アパートも世帯ごとに分割し、ぜんぶ小さな家として建てたのである。敷地模型の上に、大小8つの発泡スチロールのヴォリュームを家に見立て、並べてみた。さらに、家と家の隙間を庭として使うことができれば、それが生活上の魅力に繋がり、案を進化させることができると思った。

ちょうど同じ頃、離れを持つ住宅を別の案として考えていた。この離れは、ワンルームの小さな部屋だった。中にいても庭をいつも感じられるし、日常的に必ず庭を通るので、離れがあれば、庭が生活に欠かせないものになるだろう。そこで、8つの家に離れをつくった。つまり、建物の数をさらに増やした。アパート一室さえも、庭と離れを持つ小さな一戸建てになっていく。また、各世帯が専用の庭を持てるようにするには、建物のサイズを小さくする必要があった。このころからスタディは、模型を主体に進めるようになっていった。発泡スチロールをさらに細かく刻み、白い小さなかけらを10個、11個と増やしていく。3種類の住宅は、敷地模型の上にバラバラと散っていった。各々がいろんな大きさや形をしていて、もしかするとこれが誰かのキッチンかもしれないとか、このあたりがこの人の庭ではないかとか、どの部分を誰が使うのかと予想していく。一方、案外ぜんぶ森山さんの所有する離れの集まりとも言えてしまう気がした。模型はなんだかよくわからない集まりになった。機能を割り当てながら部屋の配列を一つひとつスタディしていくのだが、そのわりには次の日になると、どこがどれだったのか忘れてしまうような模型ばかりできた。そのうち新しい模型をまずつくってから、その使い方を考えてみたりした。すると、段々と建築の存在自体が、ひとつのランドスケープのようなものに変わり始めた。それは、どこかの巨大遺跡みたいに風化しやすいものが消え、もとの造形の意味や形式が希薄に感じられるほど断片化し、少し風通しが良くなった状態。断片化されてもどこか統一感があって、一つひとつがどうなっているかなど気にはならず、一目であるひとつの世界に見えた瞬間だった。

この模型が建築になると何が起こるのか、考えてみた。とりあえず、中が覗けるほどの大きな模型をつくった。そして、道際に建ついちばん手前のヴォリュームに、巨大な開口を開けてみた。開口が大きいことによって、道路や庭も生活の一部に使えると開放的で快適ではないかと思った。一つひとつの建物が小さいせいか、覗くと中が丸見えで、そこの生活に呑み込まれそうになった。敷地の奥の建物は、巨大遺跡のように、向こうの山脈のようにぼやけて見えた。模型のいろんな場所を覗くために、コンパクトカメラを突っ込んで写真を撮って眺めたりもした。明るい場所や暗い場所、ヴォリュームが立ちはだかったり、いきなり中が丸見えだったり、やけに向こうまで見通せたり、バラバラに建っているために部屋の中からもこの建築の全体像を見渡せるのが新鮮だった。建築物の単一性が徐々に解体されていくような感触を持った。巨大な開口をさらに数多く開けた。視線が建物を貫通するように窓を開けると、敷地の奥の部屋からも、道や隣の民家や空が見通せた。断片化は著しく加速した。大きな模型は、いっそうスカスカになり、風通しがやけによく見えた。

このようにして、森山邸は実際に建つことになる。最近は窓を全部開け放しておくと、ネコが建物を通り抜けることもあるらしい。そういえば竣工直後も、角地に建っているためか、この建物群の隙間を縫って近所の自転車がショートカットして走り去って行ったこともあった。いつも静かな森山さんは、その時すこし興奮していた。

A Landscape Like Building

Ippei Takahashi, Office of Ryue Nishizawa

How we planned Moriyama House in Tokyo: Moriyama House is in an old residential area. The people and the buildings there are open and one ordinarily hears neighbors standing and chattering to each other, alongside other noises of the city. Our client, Moriyama-san, ran a liquor shop in this neighborhood and knows these voices. Moriyama-san's design request included the desire to rebuild the liquor shop, while also building a house for his friend and some additional apartments on the one site.

At the beginning of the study, these three typologies were integrated into one volume. However, the building that came out of these studies looked like a typical massive structure. Since the site is a corner plot, the mass was conspicuously bigger than any of the other surrounding buildings. It felt like a closed building with its interior veiled in mystery, a place where an unspecified number of people entered and left. In short, it felt like the construction did not fit the open-mindedness that defines the area. Thus, I came up with a plan where the all dwellings were built as individual houses. The apartments were redesigned as small blocks. Eight houses, small and large, were laid on the site. I thought that the space between buildings could be used as gardens, creating an open lifestyle on the site.

While I was developing this idea, I thought about another option, a residence with an annex. When moving between the structures the residents would experience the garden. Such an annex would generally be like a tiny apartment, where the residents could always sense the garden around them. So I combined these two ideas, providing an annex for each of the eight residences. In other words, the number of the buildings was increased. Even one small apartment could be a single house with a garden and an annex. In order to provide each household with a private garden the size of the buildings needed to be reduced. From this stage, our study progressed based on models. Polystyrene foam was chopped into small pieces; ten, eleven, and even more tiny white blocks were created. The three kinds of houses were fragmented even more on the site model. Using the variously shaped pieces, I was wondering how each area would be used, "this could be someone's kitchen," and "this area could be the garden of this resident," but these various pieces also appeared to be an ambiguous collective of annexes owned by Moriyama-san. As I studied the arrangement of the rooms one by one, using the models and allocating functions, the models I created were so similar that the next day I could not remember which piece was where. At that time, I created a new model and considered how to use it in a new way. In doing so, I came to see that the design itself was gradually turning into a singular landscape. This was a state where those things that fade with time, like relics of an immense monument, disappear and are broken up, such that the meaning of the original form and style is no longer visible. Thus the entire form itself became light and insubstantial. Although each piece of the model was fragmented, there was a strong feeling of unity, which did not cause us to worry about what each individual piece was like. As I came to understand this sensation, I realized that I could capture the atmosphere of the design with a single glance.

Next, I began to consider what would happen if the model became an architectural structure. We created a study model, which was large enough to allow us to see the interior. As a start, I made large openings facing the roads and gardens in the volumes. I imagined that utilizing the outdoor space as a part of the residences could create an open and enjoyable feeling for the people inside. To examine the various spaces, I put a compact camera into the model and took pictures to study in depth. I saw light places, dark places, places where the volume towers over, and places where I could view the whole interior of a certain space from outside. Since the dwellings were separated, the residents in each room might experience the overall image of the site. Each place and each room were unique and I felt that every structure was both singular and part of the whole. Many more large openings were provided. Fragmentation accelerated significantly. When we opened the windows to let sight lines penetrate the building, the roads, the adjacent houses and sky, the model truly looked airy and breezy.

森山邸
Moriyama House, 2002-2005

平面図。森山さん宅は竣工時ではA〜D棟の四棟のみだが、その後徐々に拡大し最終的には敷地全体が森山邸になる予定

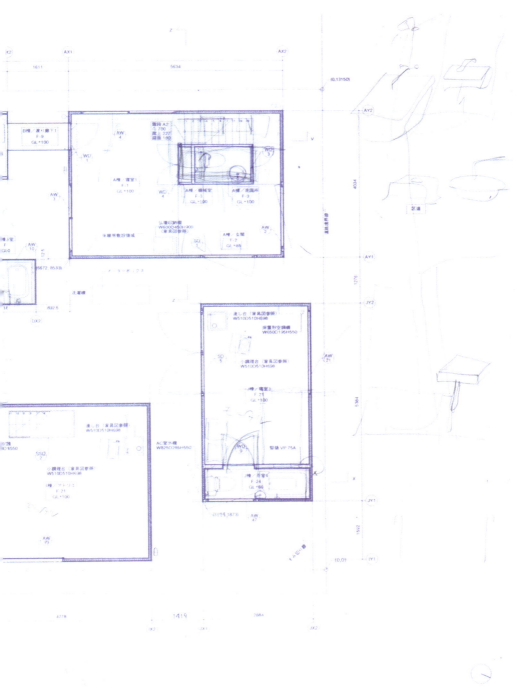

Floor plan. At first Moriyama-san will occupy only building A-D. Over time he can gradually take over the whole site

立面スケッチ。建物それぞれが流れるように立ち並ぶ/ Volumes floating together

すき間に木を植えて、緑と混ざり合う / Trees in the gaps

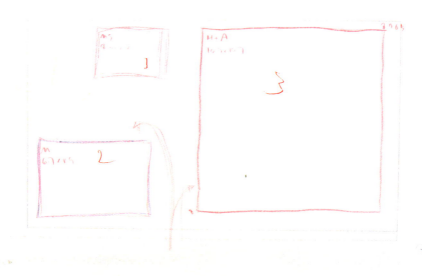

3棟案。離れ付きの自宅（1,2）とそれ以外（3）／ Moriyama-san's house with an annex (1,2) and apartments (3)

8棟案。ぜんぶ一戸建てで並べる／ Build a single dwelling for each person

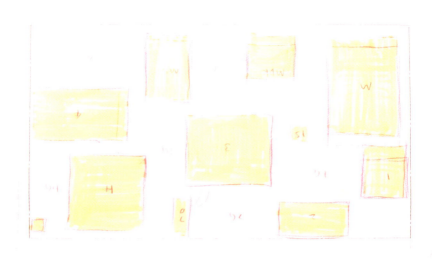

10棟案。離れを持つ6世帯が群がる / 6 households with scattered annexes

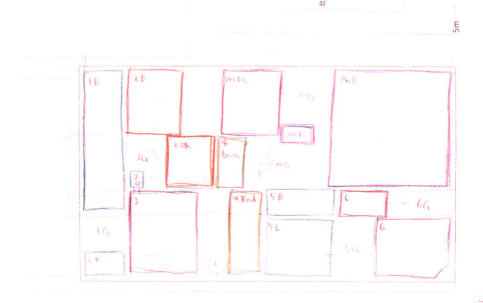

15棟案。数を増やし、庭を整理した案 / Many volumes arranged to organize the shape of the garden

41

都市と氷山

髙橋一平／西沢立衛建築設計事務所

　高さ21メートルの巨大な氷山状のヴォリュームが、住宅街に建っている。氷山は透けていて、中は木々で覆われている。小さな鎮守の森を三角の結界で囲ったような存在の、巨大で静けさを持った建築。森山邸のスタディ中に考えていた別の案である。この街には神社や民家の庭に、小さな雑木林がいくつも点在し、一度に開発した街とは異なる豊かな時間軸が存在する。建築もそういう林のような存在になってみてはどうか、と思ってつくった。そういう建築があることによって、街がいっそう文化的な環境になれば良いと思った。

　この氷山状の集合住宅は、これほどの高さをもちながら、平屋で上空へ高く吹抜けている。つまり巨大なワンルームである。内部は雨も入り風も抜けて、森のように木が生い茂っている。アパートの各部屋は、地下に埋まっている。各部屋はそれぞれアリの巣のように有機的な形状に掘り込まれている。かつ、地上に離れの小さい部屋を持ち、住人は地上と地下を行き来しながら生活する。例えば、地上の森で食事をし、地下の洞窟で眠る。このほか、バスルームが森にある部屋や、森で眠る部屋もある。森山さんは、地上で犬を飼い、時々訪れる近くの人々や、アパートの住人と食事や会話をする。森はそういう場所である。そして、上空には森山さんのロフトがある。どこも眺めが良く、日光浴のできるテラスやお風呂、星空に囲まれて眠るベッドなどがある。このように、天空と森を移動するオーナーと、森と洞窟を移動するアパートの住人たちがやわらかな棲み分けをしながら共同で暮らす、ひとつの生態系のような集合住宅である。

City and Iceberg

Ippei Takahashi, Office of Ryue Nishizawa

　This is another idea I was thinking about while studying Moriyama House. In this neighborhood there are many small groves with tress scattered among the shrines and private residences, giving the substantial history. In my design I was wondering what a building that resembled these groves would feel like. I hoped that such architecture would contribute to the history of the area while fitting into the existing texture.

　Although this iceberg-like apartment building is very tall, it remains a single-storey dwelling with its high ceiling reaching to the sky. Trees bristle up as in a forest. On the other hand, each room is buried in the ground, creating an organic shape like an ant's nest. There are also small annexes above ground. The residents would live their lives meandering up and down, moving between underground and above. For example, they may have a meal in the forest above and sleep in a cave below. In addition, there is a loft for Moriyama-san up in the air. The loft has a wonderful 360-degree view, with a terrace and a bathtub. This collective concept is formed like an ecological system, with the owner moving from the forest to the sky and the residents of the apartments moving from the forest to cave, living loosely separated communal lives.

氷山形のスタディ模型 / Iceberg studies

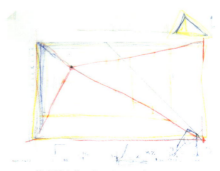

等高線を使ったスタディ / Contour lines

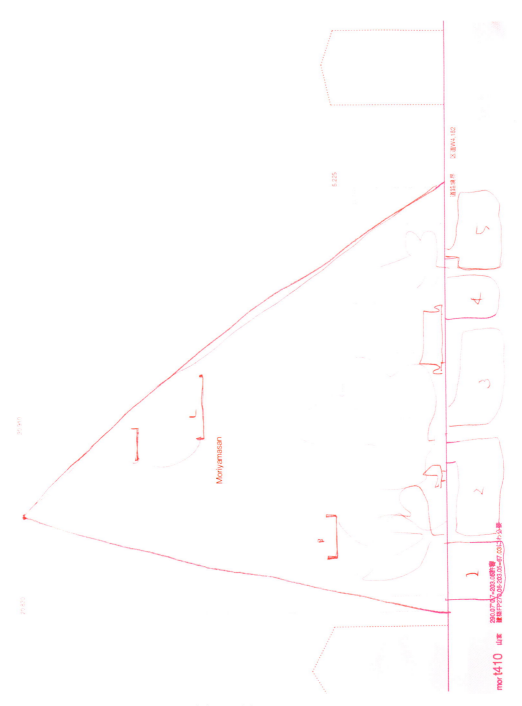

断面スケッチ / Section sketch

十和田市現代美術館
Towada Art Center, 2005-2008

街の中心を走る官庁街通り全体を美術館に見立てるという構想のもと、通り沿いの空き地の一角に建てられた美術館。アートと都市、建築の融合をめざす。

It is built on one of the empty lots left in the master-plan of Towada's main street, which runs through the middle of the town. The entire street is envisioned as a museum.

a 美術館敷地 / Site of the art museum
b 官庁街通り / Main street
c 空地にアート作品を置く / Placing artwork in an empty lot
d 通りの床仕上げを統一する / Unify the road surfaces

通り全体を美術館に見立てる街づくりのアイディア
Idea for community development

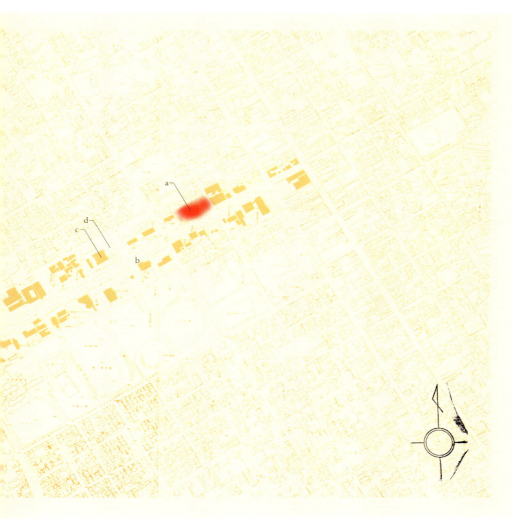

街の全体図。江戸時代末期に開拓された歴史的街区で、格子状の道路網がのびやかに広がっているのがわかる
A historical town block developed at the end of the Edo period. A lattice like road network stretches over the site

a 美術館敷地／Site of the museum
b 官庁街通り／Main street
c 公共施設／Public facilities
d 空地／Empty lots
e 稲生川／Inaoi River

十和田市現代美術館　Towada Art Center

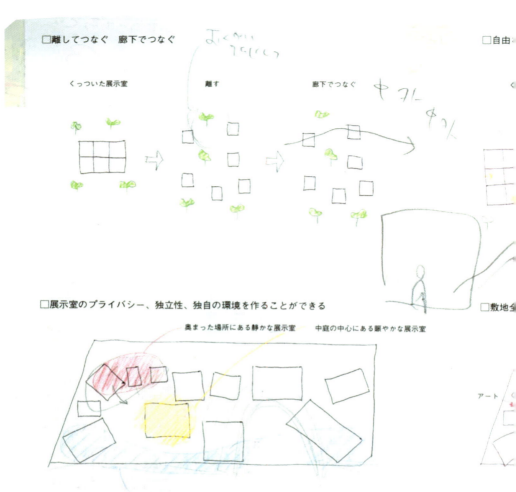

コンペ提出用ダイアグラムのスタディ。大きく伸びる廊下で展示室どうしをつなぎ、広場や庭をつくる
Connecting the exhibition rooms with hallways creating open spaces and gardens

アートと建築が混ざり合う集落 / Art and Architecture like a settlement

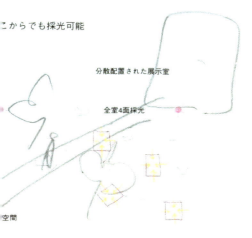

模型スタディの風景 / Study model

作品の多くが恒久展示作品であるため、展示室をバラバラにして、各々を独立させた。各室は作品サイズに合わせて自由に形をつくることができる。展示室は独立パビリオンみたいなもので、それらは渡り廊下でつながる。
As most of the artworks are to be on permanent display, the exhibition rooms are separated and built independently. Each room is formed freely according to the size of the artwork. The exhibition rooms are like independent pavilions, joined together by connecting passages.

House A, 2004-2006

密集した住宅地に建つ住宅。都心で、楽園のような住宅をつくろうと考えた。最初に考えたのは、巨大なワンルームの植物園のような庭のような案。
A home built in a densely populated residential area. I thought of creating a paradise-like dwelling. My initial idea was a huge one-room botanical garden or yard.

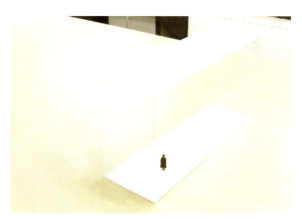

巨大な空間で、ガラスで囲まれている
A huge space surrounded by glass

ガラスの大空間は、屋根が開く。樹木が木陰をつくり出す
The roof of the huge glass space opens. The trees create leafy shadows

House A

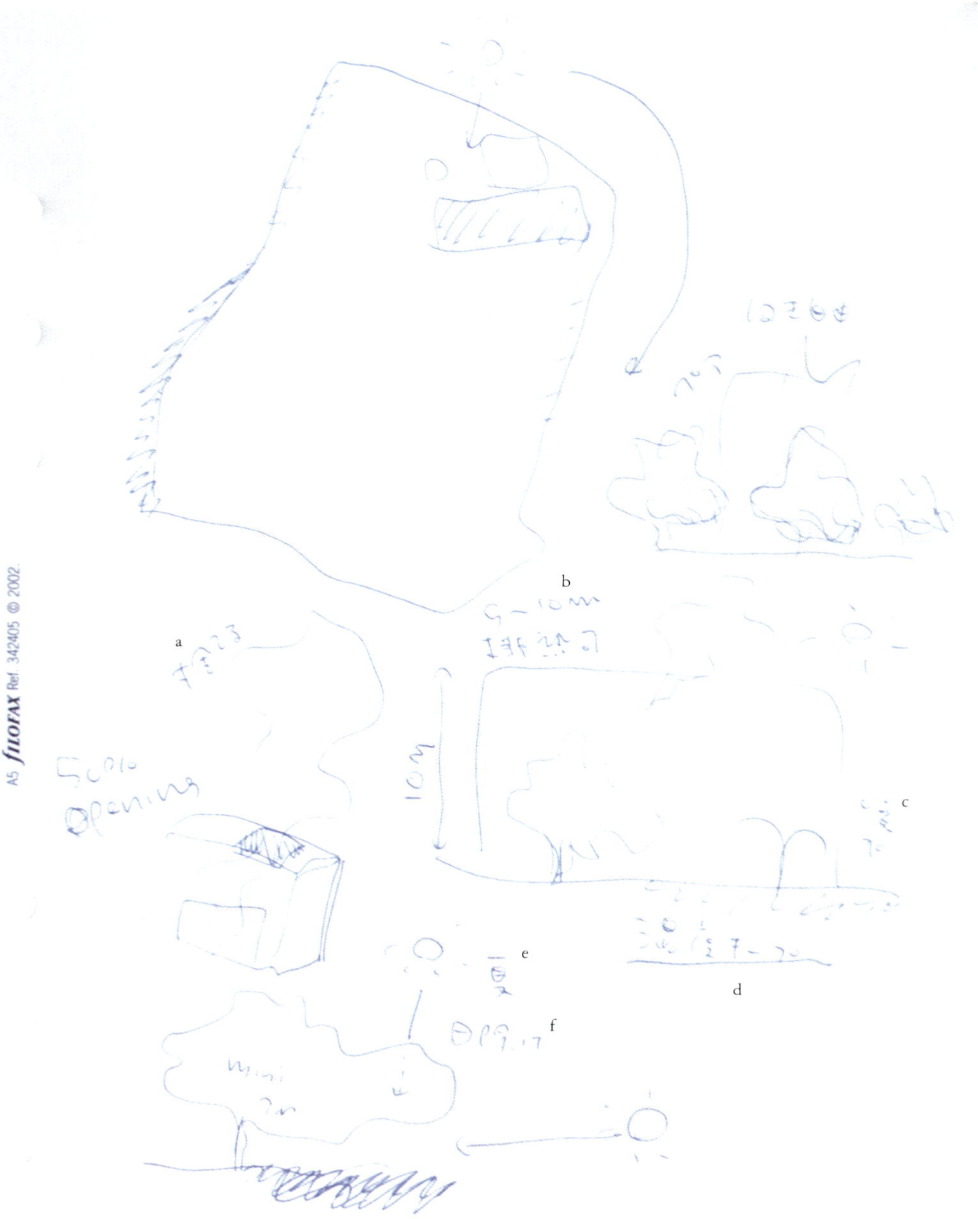

a 熱を捨てる／Junk heat
b 排熱／Exhaust heat
c 噴水／Fountain
d 湿度をキープ／Maintain the humidity
e 夏／Summer
f 日除け／Shade

環境エンジニアとの議論メモ。快適な室内環境をつくり出す
Creating a comfortable indoor environment with an environmental engineer

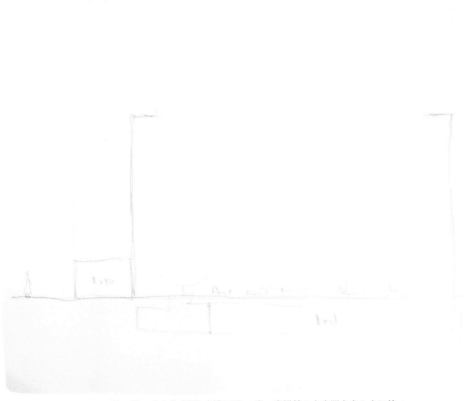

第34案。大きな空間に屋根がない案。半屋外の大空間を真ん中に持つ
Plan No.34. Plan of a large space without a roof, with a large and semi-outdoor space in the middle

部屋がズレながらつながっていくことで、大きなワンルーム空間をつくり出す。ズレることで中と外が連続する。
By connecting misaligned rooms, a large one-room space is created. This misalignment makes the interior and exterior continuous.

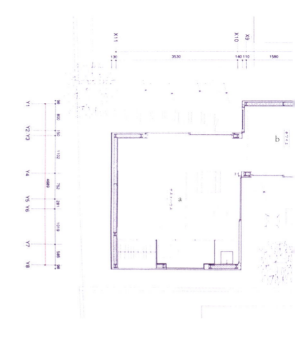

a ゲストルーム / Guest room
b ホワイエ / Foyer
c サンルーム / Sunroom
d ダイニングキッチン / Dining kitchen
e バスリビング / Bathroom

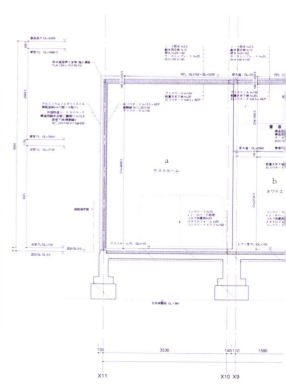

庭のような室内風景 / Indoor landscape like a garden

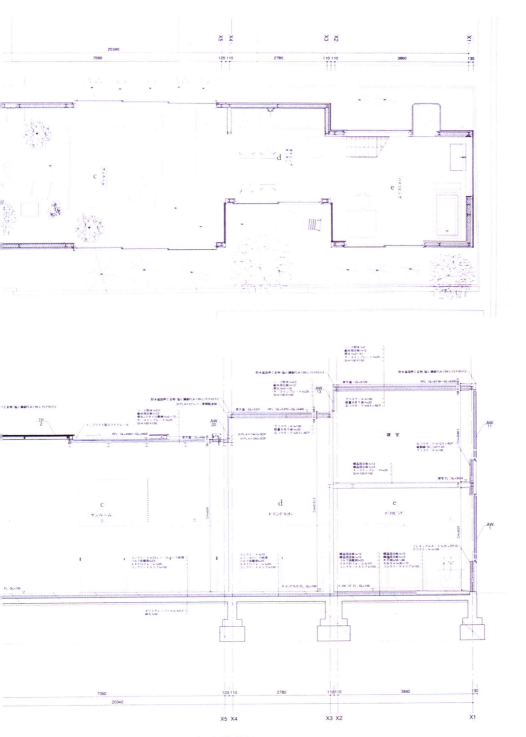

平面図と断面図 / Floor plan and section

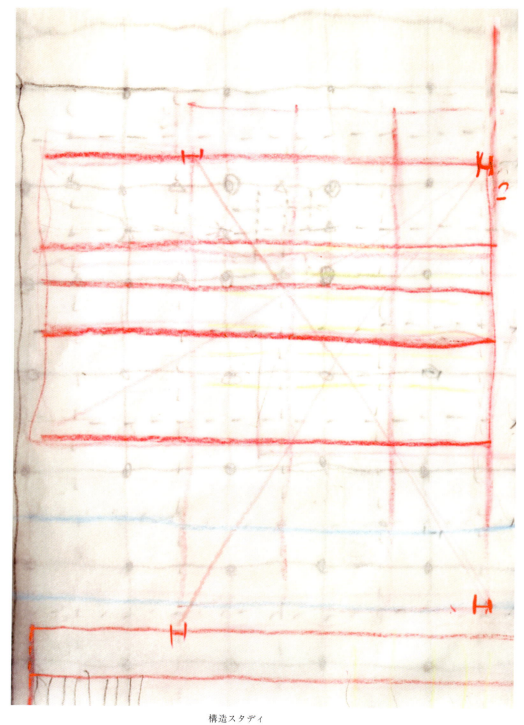

構造スタディ
Structural study

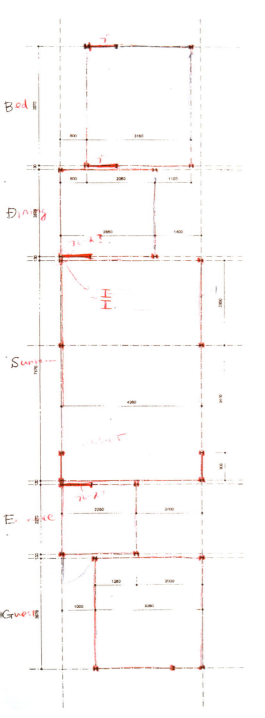

細く透明な鉄骨フレームが連続していく
Continuous thin and transparent steel frames

透明で開放性のある構造を目指した。壁構造ではなく、柱と梁で考えた。全体が100ミリの鋼材でできている。フレームが繊細であることで、透明で、かつ明るい庭のような室内を生み出す。

We examined the idea of using columns and beams rather than a wall structure. The entire structure is made of 100mm structural steel columns. The delicate frames broaden the site and create an indoor environment that feels like a bright garden.

Before | After

Through design, I would like to consider the shape architecture will take in the new age. Since a new architecture is assumed to exist as required by the new age, I would like to reflect on the form of this architecture that will make us feel the values of the new age. However, the field of architectural design does not necessarily deal with such wide and abstract issues but rather deals far more often with concrete and realistic issues. For example, it has to respond to various types of concrete issues, such as where the kitchen should whether two-storeys or three-storeys is better? Most of such issues are concrete and realistic, rather than abstract and imaginary.

The issue of "surrounding environment" is, to put it briefly, mainly related to the layout planning of architecture, such as how the architecture of a building should relate to those on either side and in the neighbourhood, or how the structure is to be placed. I believe the term "program" may have several meanings, but briefly speaking, it is a matter of how architectural space is to be used. These two issues are fairly important elements when proceeding with the study of design. This has not changed in a long time. To me, these were simply individual concrete issues at first, as well as being realistic technical issues to be solved using design techniques. However, after having experience of several projects, I gradually came to understand that these two issues were also somewhat wider and bigger issues.

30

中も外もない状態。庭にも見えるし、室内にも見える空間
The space can be seen both as a garden and the interior of the structure

風と光が溢れる、明るく透明な空間
Bright and transparent space full of wind and light

モントリオールの展覧会
CCA exhibition, 2008

カナダ、モントリオールで行なわれた展覧会。ガーデンアンドハウス、House A、森山邸がそれぞれ一室ずつに展示された。
Exhibition held in Montreal, Canada. Garden and House, House A, and Moriyama House were each exhibited in one room.

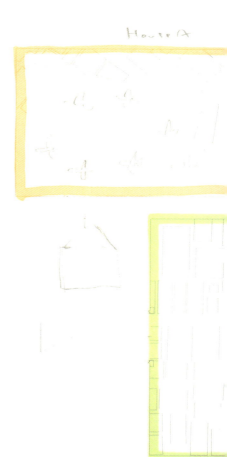

地元の新聞記事 / Article from local newspaper

a 森山邸、外観 / Moriyama House, External view
b House A、浴室 / House A, Bathroom
c House A、サンルーム / House A, Sunroom

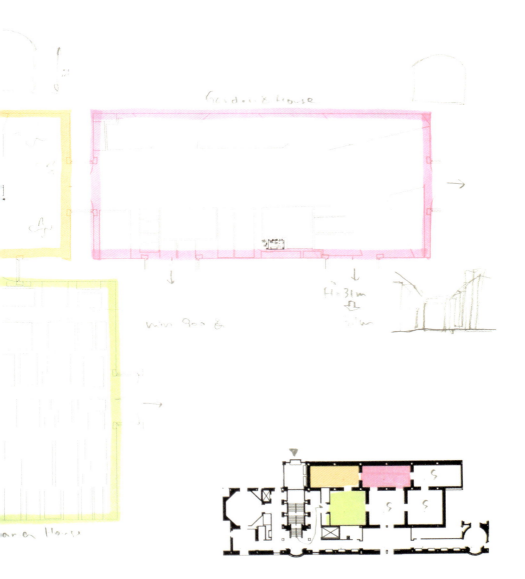

会場構成スタディ案のひとつ。3つの住宅について周辺の街を含めた巨大な模型を各展示室に配分する
One of the study plans. A huge model of each the three dwellings is allocated to each exhibition room

モントリオールの展覧会／CCA exhibition　59

エモナホテル
Emona Hotel, 2006-

F フロント / Front desk
R レストラン / Restaurant
B 朝食室 / Breakfast room
P プール / Swimming pool
O オーナーの家 / Owner's residence
G 野原 / Field
1-9 客室 / Guest rooms
10 岬の突端のスイート
　　Suites at the tip of the cape

村の地図。客室が村に散らばる
Map of the village. All of the hotel rooms are scattered

1. 集落案 / Settlement Plan

黒海に面した村に小さなホテルを建てる。美しい自然と海に囲まれた、ソフィアから車で5時間の村。スタディの第一案は、村全体に客室が点在するという案だった。村とホテルが混ざる。

The project is to build a small hotel in a village fronting the Black Sea. Located amidst beautiful natural scenery and near the ocean. The first plan for the study is to sprinkle the guest rooms all over the village. The hotel will intermingle with the village.

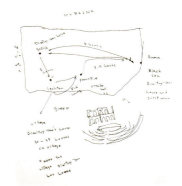

エモナまでの道のり / Road to Emona

村の中に客室やフロント、食事室が点在する
Guest rooms, the front desk and the breakfast room are scattered around the village

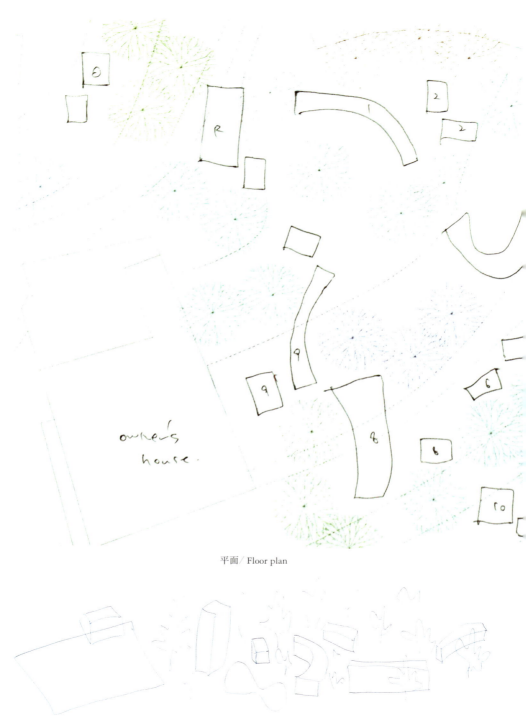

平面/ Floor plan

立面/ Elevation

模型/ Model

2. フォレスト案/ Forest Plan

森の中に、いろいろな形をした10の客室群が散らばる、分散型コテージホテル。書斎やバスルームが離れとなっている客室もある。この村には森がないので、森からつくらなければならない。木々と建築が混ざり合う。
A cottage-type hotel with ten variously shaped guest rooms scattered amidst the forest. Some guest rooms have an annex study room or bathroom. There was no forest in this village. We need to create the forest first. The trees and the architecture will intermingle.

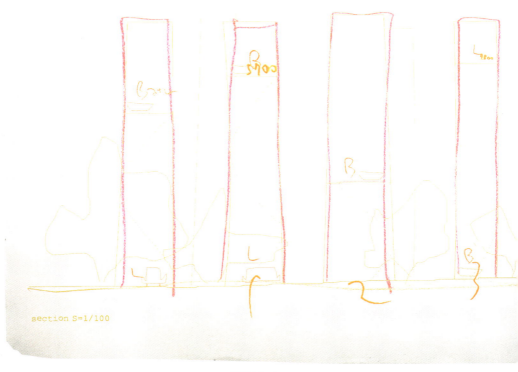

断面 / Section

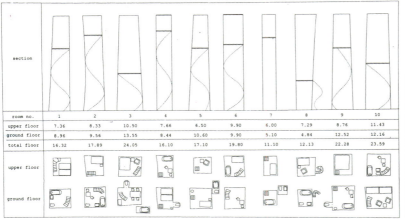

section										
room no.	1	2	3	4	5	6	7	8	9	10
upper floor	7.36	8.33	10.50	7.66	6.50	9.90	6.00	7.29	8.76	11.43
ground floor	8.96	9.56	13.55	8.44	10.60	9.90	5.10	4.84	12.52	12.16
total floor	16.32	17.89	24.05	16.10	17.10	19.80	11.10	12.13	22.28	23.59
upper floor										
ground floor										

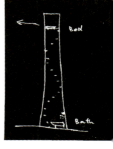

客室の概要表 / Overview of guest room

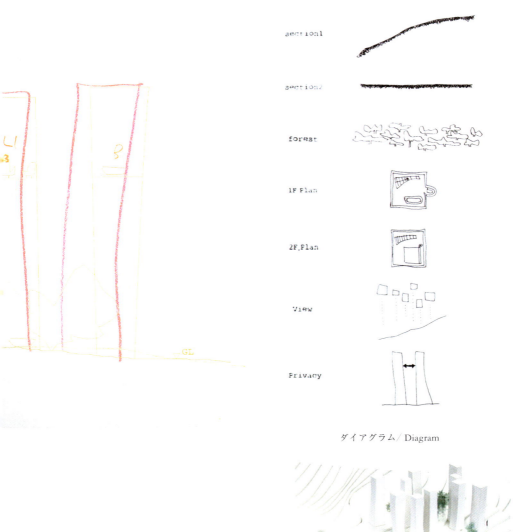

ダイアグラム / Diagram

模型 / Model

3. タワー案 / Tower Plan

各客室がタワー状になって、林立する案。各タワーは木々に囲まれた地上階と、林より高く持ち上げられた空中階の両方を持つことができる。

Each guest room is in the form of a tower bristling up into the air. Each tower is made up of two floors aboveground surrounded by trees. The higher floor is elevated above the forest.

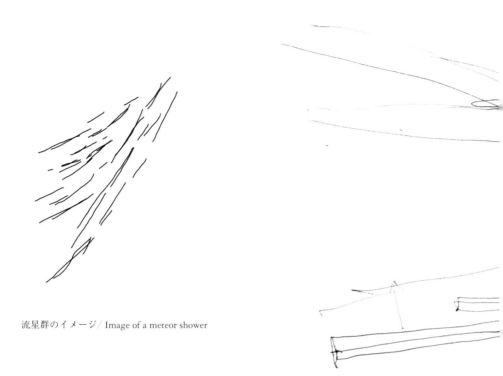

流星群のイメージ / Image of a meteor shower

4. スター案 / Star Plan
細長い客室を、等高線に沿って分散配置する。眺望確保のためにずれながら並んでゆき、全体として流星群のような配置となる。

The slender guest houses are dispersed along the contours. They are not aligned in order to ensure a view, instead allocated like a meteor shower that has come down on the on the whole site.

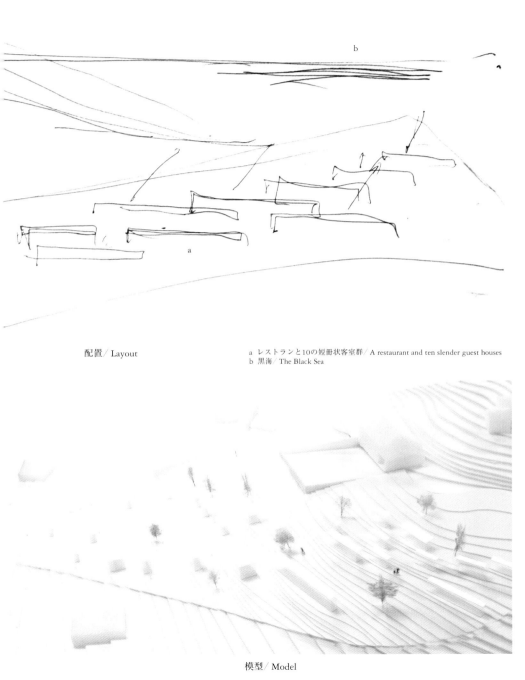

配置／Layout

a レストランと10の短冊状客室群／A restaurant and ten slender guest houses
b 黒海／The Black Sea

模型／Model

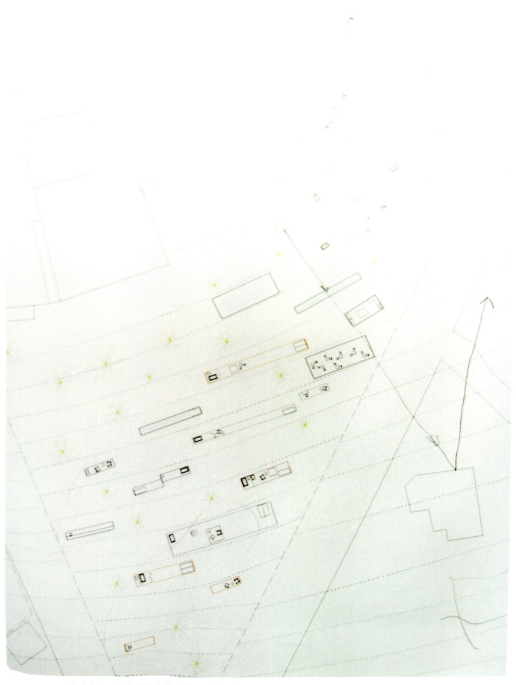

たくさんの客室が等高線に沿って並ぶ/ Many guest houses allocated along the contours

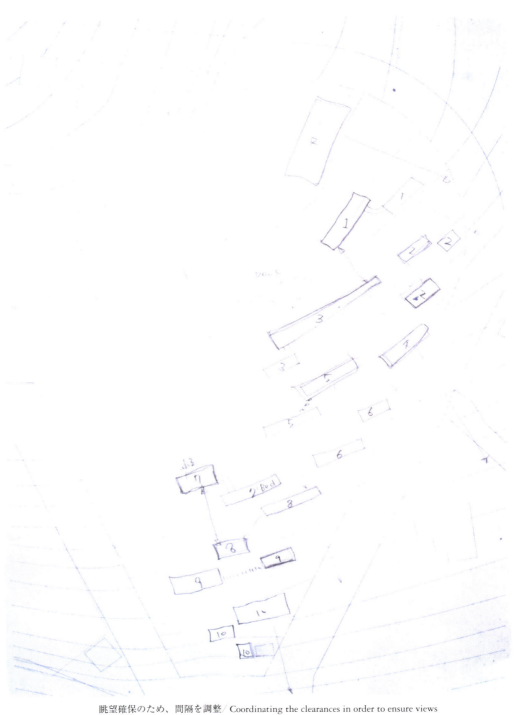

眺望確保のため、間隔を調整 / Coordinating the clearances in order to ensure views

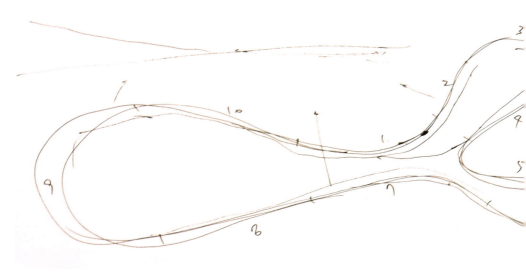

配置計画 / Site plan

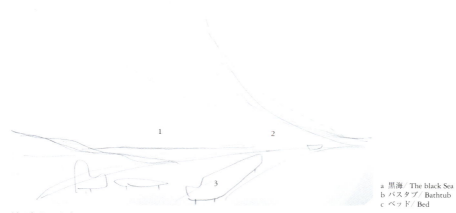

ゲストルーム / Guest room

a 黒海 / The black Sea
b バスタブ / Bathtub
c ベッド / Bed

断面スタディ / Study of the section

模型/ Model

5. リング案/ Ring Plan

10の客室が帯状に連なり、ぐるっと一周して庭を囲む。なだらかな斜面の上でおおらかなカーブを描く。建物は地形に合わせてカーブし、中庭型ながらどの部屋からも海が見える形状になっている。斜面にべったり張りつく建築で、客室床はスロープ部分が多い。

Ten guest houses lie in a band around the garden, with soft curves on gentle slopes. All the guest houses curve in accordance with the geography of the site and have access to ocean views. This construction follows the contours. The floors of the guest houses are mostly sloped.

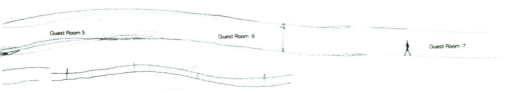

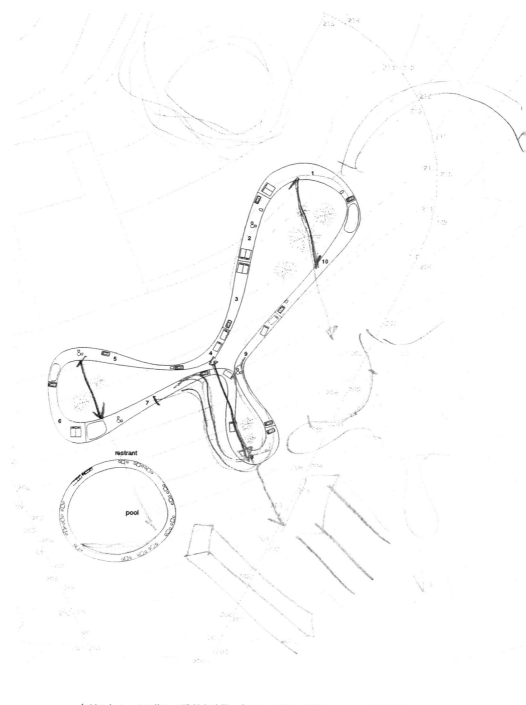

全ゲストルームの海への眺望を確保。向かいの部屋と距離をとって、形が変わっていく
All the guest rooms are ensured an ocean view. They have different shapes with distance to the opposite guest rooms

ゲストルームごとのプランと高低差のスタディ
The plan for each guest room and a study on the differences in elevation

エモナホテル Emona Hotel

小山登美夫ギャラリー代官山
TKG Daikanyama, 2007

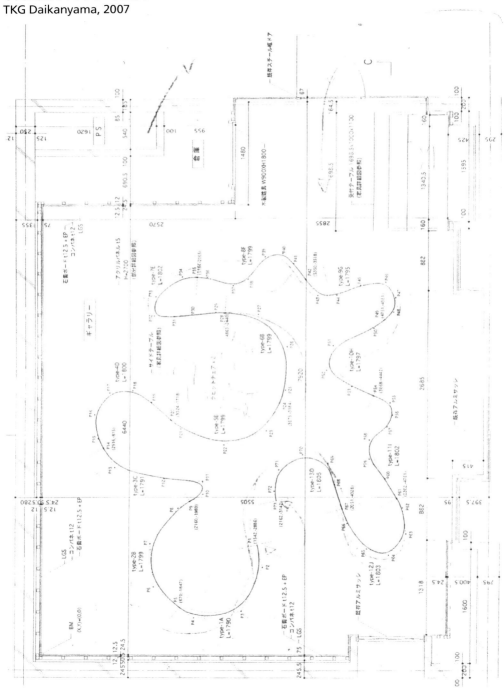

花のような平面形をしたアクリルが、カーブしながら空間をつくってゆく
Curving acrylic in plan creates many different spaces

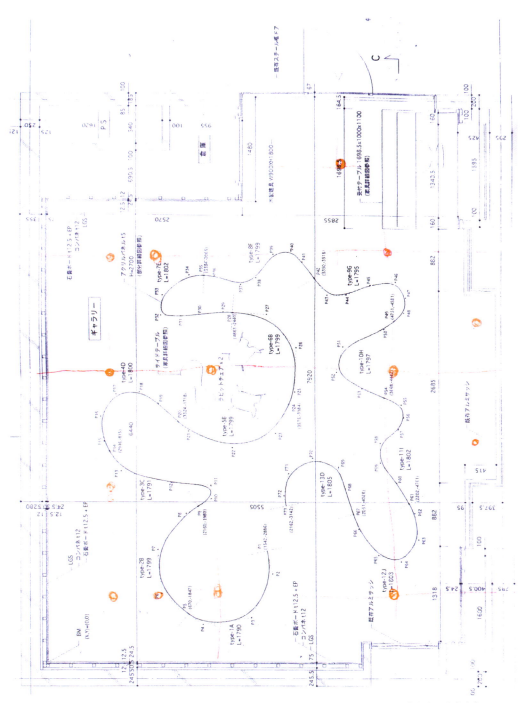

アクリルの大きな塊が部屋中央にでんと置かれる。大きいが存在があいまいで、あるようなないようなもの
This transparent piece is ambiguous. It might exist and it might not

永井画廊
Nagai Garou, 2008

画廊のファサードスタディ。透明アクリル製の窓を考えた。この窓は全体がひとつの大きなレンズになっていて、画廊の中が拡大されて見える。人や絵のプロポーションが歪む。
Study of the gallery facade. The idea is to use a transparent acrylic window. It acts a large lens, which magnifies the interior of the gallery. The figures of people and paintings are deformed.

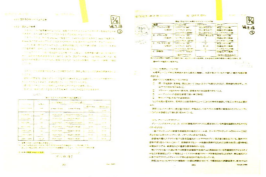
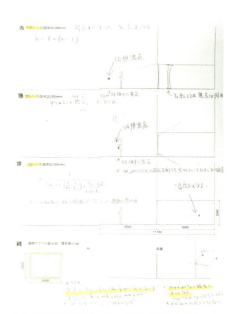

レンズは最大で120ミリ飛び出す
The lens protrudes by a maximum of 120mm

レンズの片側が平らであれば焦点が遠くなり安全
One side of the lens is flat

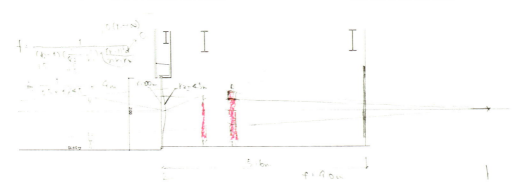

像の拡大率、焦点距離を作図で検討 / Examining the magnification of the statue in relation to the focal distance

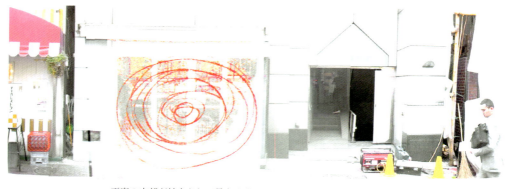

画廊の内部が拡大されて見える / The interior of the gallery is magnified

アクリル板を形状に合わせて重ねて削り、レンズをつくる
Lay acrylic plates before grinding

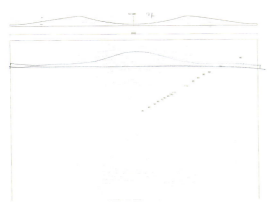

等高線で形状スタディ
Study of a form using contour lines

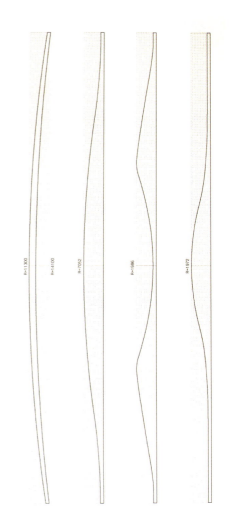

形状の検討案、断面図 / Study section

磨いていく / Polishing

レンズ窓を嵌めたところ / Looking through window

熊本駅東口駅前広場
Kumamoto Terminal, 2007-

雲のような形をしたいくつもの屋根が空中に浮かび、人々のための都市空間をつくり出す。各ゾーンとも、バス停車場やタクシー乗降場などの地上レヴェルの機能配置、動線の流れをそのまま形に写し取って、有機的な屋根形状が生まれた。複数の屋根はコンクリートの薄い版によってつくられ、お互いに関係しあいながら雲のように浮かぶ。水平方向は壁がなく、まったく透明な都市空間が生まれる。

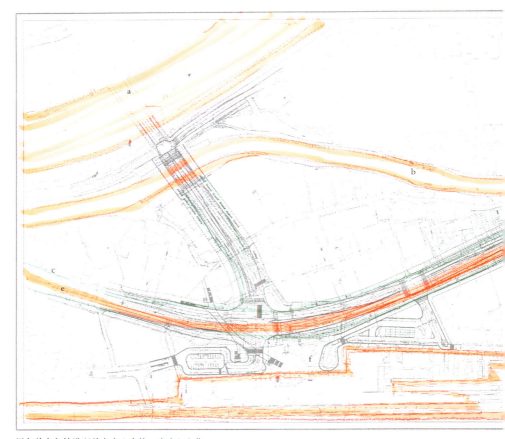

川と並木と鉄道が並走する自然に恵まれた街
Town richly endowed with nature, where a river, a line of trees, and railroads run side by side

Many roofs shaped like clouds float in the air, creating public spaces. By shaping the functional layout of the ground level for the bus stop and taxi stand, the flow of dynamic lines creates organic roof forms. The multiple roofs, made of thin concrete plates, float like clouds, interrelating with one another. There are no walls and thus a totally transparent urban space is generated.

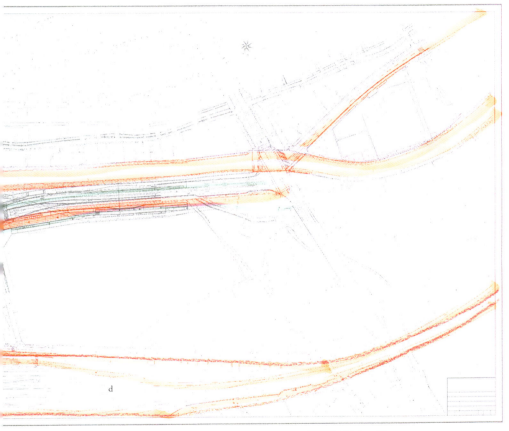

a 白川 / The Shirakawa River
b 坪井川 / The Tsuboigawa River
c 主要地方道高森線 / Principal Prefectural Road
d JR鹿児島本線 / JR Kagoshima Line
e 熊本市電 / Kumamoto City Tram
f 熊本駅東口広場 / Kumamoto Station East Entrance Square

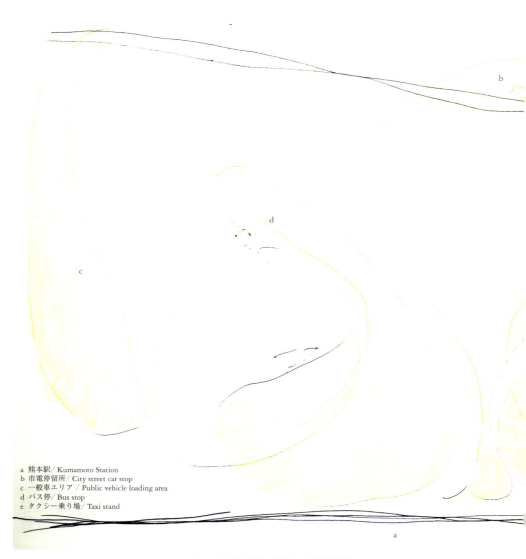

a 熊本駅／Kumamoto Station
b 市電停留所／City street car stop
c 一般車エリア／Public vehicle loading area
d バス停／Bus stop
e タクシー乗り場／Taxi stand

ゾーニングに応じて複数の屋根を架ける
Several roofs reflect the zoning

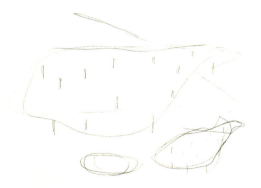

さまざまな屋根が広場に浮かぶ
Various roofs floating in the station square

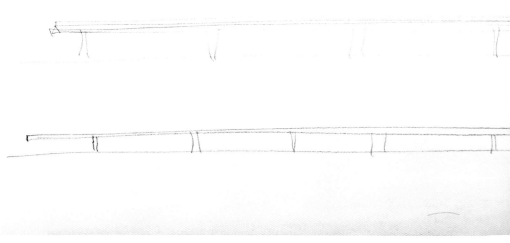

屋根厚、プロポーションの検討／Examining the thickness and the proportions of the roof

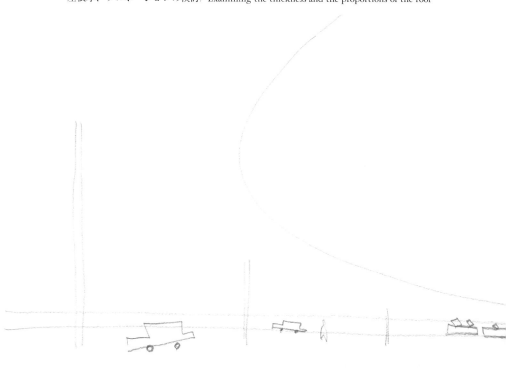

おおらかに伸びる屋根／Broad extensive roof

屋根群は、既存街並みと調和しながらも、いままで熊本駅前になかったような都市空間をつくり出す。人、自動車、電車、あらゆるものが往来する大屋根の空間。
The group of roofs not only harmonizes with the face of the existing street, but also creates an urban space which has not been seen in station square. A space under large roofs where everything - people, bicycles, and trains - come and go.

俯瞰／Bird's-eye view

模型／Model

熊本駅東口駅前広場 Kumamoto Terminal

軽井沢研究所
k-project, 2007-

軽井沢に計画されている、企業のための研究所。絵画展示とともに、レクチャー場やカフェ、ホワイエなどが一室空間に並ぶ。緩やかに傾斜した床の上に、3次元的にカーブした曲面屋根が浮かぶ。天井高や床レヴェルがゆっくり上下する、動的なワンルーム空間がつくられる。中庭がいくつか取られ、光と風を室内にもたらす。木々や人々、庭、絵画が、ゆるやかに混ざり合いながら、美術と自然の透明な空間をつくり出す。

A training facility for a company. A lecture hall, cafe, foyer, and a painting exhibition space are laid out in a one-room space. A roof with a three-dimensionally-curved surface floats above the gently sloped floor, creating a dynamic one-room space where the ceiling height and floor level slowly rise and fall. There are several courtyards to bring in light and wind. Trees, people, and paintings are gently intermingling with one another, creating an open space of art and nature.

広がる屋根／Expansive roof

床の傾斜／Slope of the floor

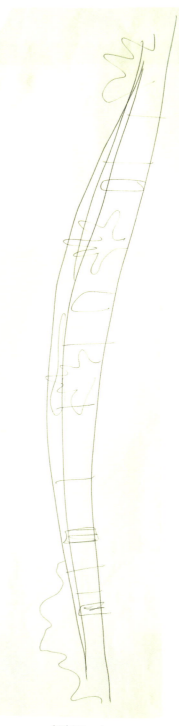

立面／Elevation

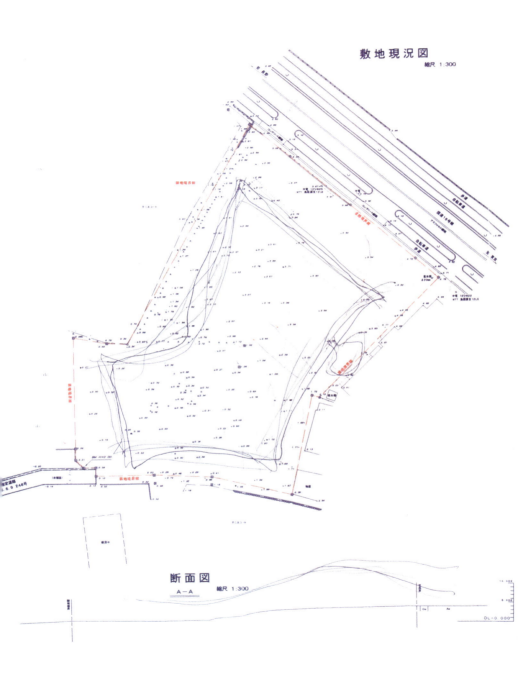

平面GL+1,500 / Floor plan GL+1,500

平面GL+4,000 / Floor plan GL+4,000

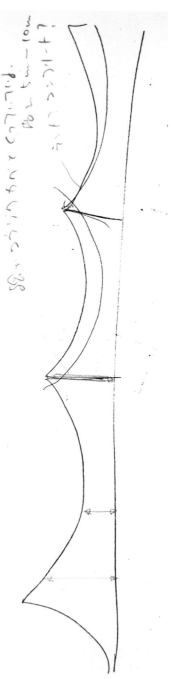

断面 / Section

初期案のひとつ。展示壁部分の屋根が稜線状につまみ上げられ、カーブした展示空間が生まれる
One of the initial plans. The roof is lifted in ridge-like lines, generating curved exhibition spaces

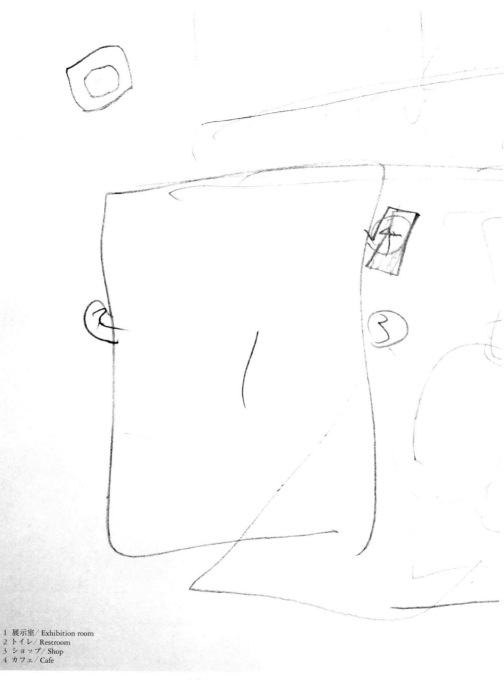

1 展示室／Exhibition room
2 トイレ／Restroom
3 ショップ／Shop
4 カフェ／Cafe

大きなワンルームの案。平面
Plan of a large studio

壁がガラスなので外周は明るい。かつ平面が大きいため映像展示が可能なほど、中央部は自然と暗くなる
One can image glass walls with a large footprint. The center becomes naturally dark and the circumference bright

a 中庭／Courtyard
b 展示室／Exhibition room
c 新しく描いた外形／Newly drawn exterior shape

敷地の形状にあわせ、敷地いっぱいに広がる
Covering the entire site, matching its geography

大きな中庭をたくさん持つ。鑑賞空間と緑を近づける
Many large courtyards, merging gallery and greenery

軽井沢研究所/k-project

最終案の初期スケッチ。水平垂直の短い線が絵を飾る壁。薄い線で中庭と樹木が描かれている
Initial draft of the current plan. A plan with short vertical and horizontal lines that highlight the paintings

その模型。壁一枚に絵画一枚が対応する。木々と絵画が交ざり合う
Model of the plan. One painting on one wall. Trees mingle with the paintings

t-project, 2004-

瀬戸内海に浮かぶ島に計画されている美術館。低いコンクリートシェルが水平方向に広がるワンルーム空間をつくり出す。美術と建築の統合、自然と人工の統合。
This is an art museum to be built on an island. A low concrete shell creates a one-room space expanding horizontally. A fusion of art and architecture, an integration of nature and art.

敷地は、瀬戸内海に浮かぶたくさんの島のひとつ / One of many islands floating in the Seto Inland Sea

瀬戸内海 / The Seto Inland Sea

012 **A**
R=20000

初期スタディ案のひとつ。山脈のような空間／One of the initial plans. A space like a mountain range

034 **E**
R=20000

トレーシングペーパーを複雑な山の形状に折る／Fold the tracing papers

018 **D**
R=20000

尾根の下に空間が生まれる / Generating a space under the paper

056 **G**
R=20000

尾根の形に沿って空間が展開する / Developing the space along with the roof shape

97

032 F

山案の発展形。今度は島の地形図を転写し、等高線を頼りに折り曲げる
The developed plan. Transcribe the map of the island onto tracing paper and fold it according to the contour lines

033 G

海の部分は、地下に空間を設ける
The sea would be underground in this shape

断面スケッチ / Sectional sketch

水滴案。おおらかなワンルームで、屋根が大きくカーブし、地面から立ち上がる。平らなシェル。
Drop plans. An open one-room space with a curving roof, rising from the ground.

水滴が集まる
Water droplets gather

大きな水滴。屋根が大きくカーブし、地面に着地する
Huge drop. The roof makes a long curve and lands

出入口を設けるため、水滴の端をつまむ
Lift the corner of the drop to create the entrance

アクリル成形モデルによる形の検証
Examining the form with an acrylic model

内観／Interior

外形／Exterior form

出入口 / Entrance

開口部 / Opening

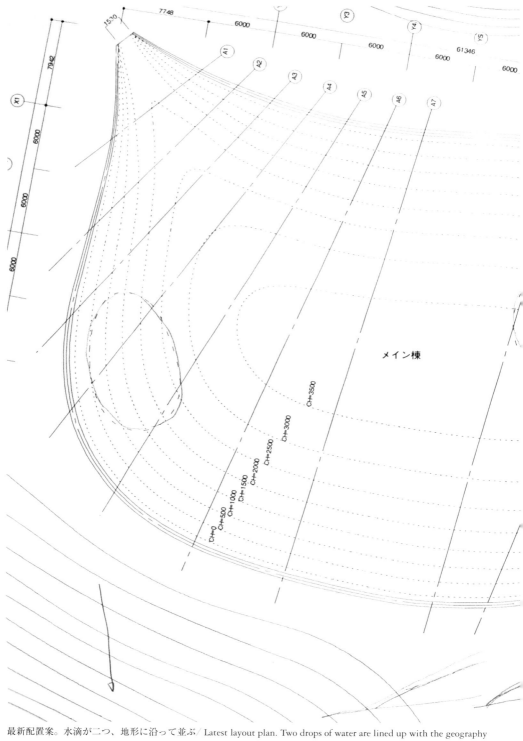

最新配置案。水滴が二つ、地形に沿って並ぶ / Latest layout plan. Two drops of water are lined up with the geography

a 人のアプローチと開口との関係 / The relationship between people's approach and openings
b 作品との関係で、二つの開口を東西軸に揃える / A set of two openings in the east and west axes, in view of the artwork

本プロジェクト
Book Project, 2008-2009

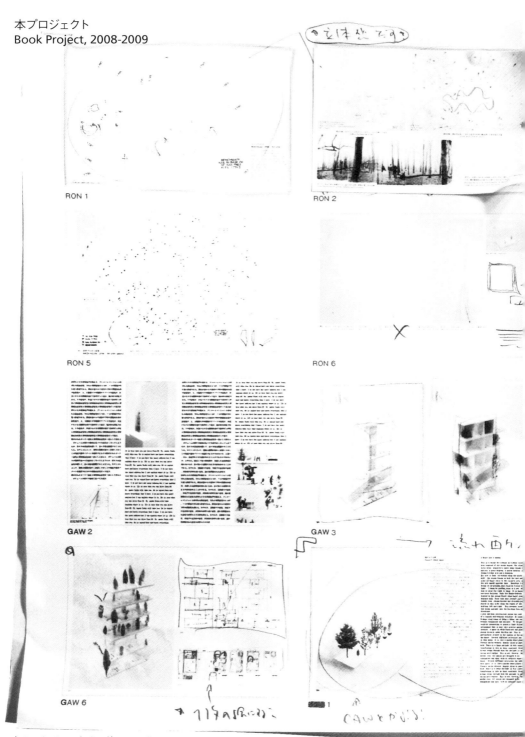

本のスタディのための絵コンテ / Storyboards for the study of this book

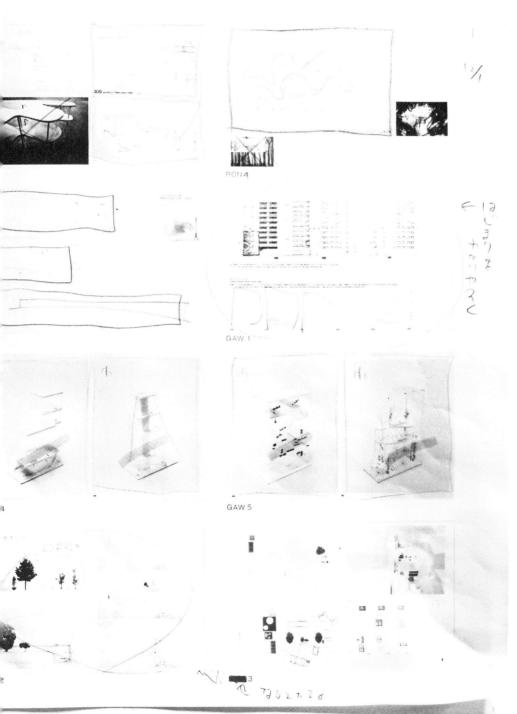

絵コンテ2/ Storyboard two

本プロジェクト Book Project

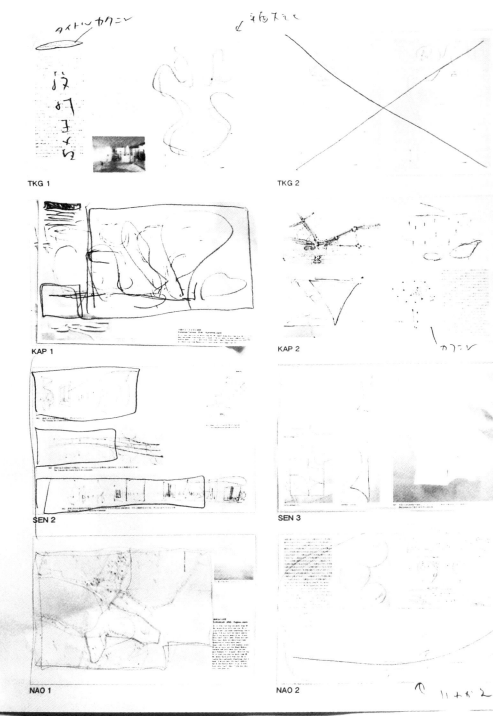

絵コンテ3/ Storyboard three

NAG 2

SEN 1

SEN 5

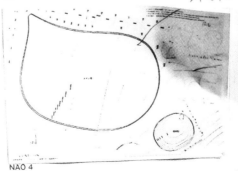

NAO 4

本プロジェクト Book Project 109

略　歴

西沢立衛／西沢立衛建築設計事務所

1966　東京都生まれ
1990　横浜国立大学大学院修士課程修了
1990　妹島和世建築設計事務所入所
1995　妹島和世と共に SANAA 設立
1997　西沢立衛建築設計事務所設立
現 在　横浜国立大学大学院建築都市スクール Y-GSA 教授

主な受賞

1998　第 50 回日本建築学会賞　《国際情報科学芸術アカデミーマルチメディア工房》
1999　第 15 回吉岡賞　《ウィークエンドハウス》
2002　アメリカ芸術文化アカデミー　アーノルド・W・ブルンナー賞
2002　ヴィンセント・スカモッツィ賞、オーストリア
2004　第 9 回ヴェネツィアビエンナーレ国際建築展金獅子賞
2005　第 46 回毎日芸術賞　《金沢 21 世紀美術館》
2005　平成 17 年度文部科学省若手科学者賞
2005　ロルフ・ショック賞、スウェーデン
2006　第 58 回日本建築学会賞　《金沢 21 世紀美術館》
2007　マリオ・パニ賞、メキシコ
2007　ベルリン芸術賞、ドイツ
2010　プリツカー賞、米国
2011　芸術文化勲章 オフィシエ、フランス
2012　第 64 回日本建築学会賞　《豊島美術館》
2012　第 25 回村野藤吾賞
2013　銀の定規賞、フランス
2014　デイライト賞、スイス
2016　イリノイ工科大学ミース・クラウン・ホール・アメリカ賞、米国

翻　訳　トーマス・ダニエル（pp.8-9）、牧尾晴喜／スタジオ OJMM（pp.10-109）
翻訳協力　サム・チェルマイエフ
制　作　西沢立衛＋髙橋一平＋藤澤賢一＋中坪多恵子／西沢立衛建築設計事務所

Profile

Ryue Nishizawa ╱ Office of Ryue Nishizawa

1966   Born in Tokyo, Japan

1990   Graduated from Yokohama National University with Master's Degree in Architecture

1990   Joined Kazuyo Sejima & Associates

1995   Established SANAA with Kazuyo Sejima

1997   Established Office of Ryue Nishizawa

2010- Professor at Graduated School of Engineering, Yokohama National University

Selected Awards

1998   The Prize of Architectural Institute of Japan, Japan

1999   The 15th Yoshioka Prize, Japan

2002   Arnold W. Brunner Memorial Prize in Architecture, American Academy of Arts & Letters, USA

2002   Architecture Award of Salzburg Vincenzo Scamozzi, Austria

2004   Golden Lion for the most remarkable work in the exhibition Metamorph
in the 9th International Architecture Exhibition, la Biennale di Venezia, Italy

2005   46th Mainichi Art Award (Architecture Category), Japan

2005   The Young Scientists' Prize, The Commendation for Science and Technology
by the Minister of Education, Culture, Sports, Science and Technology

2005   The Rolf Schock Prize in category of visual arts, Sweden

2006   The Prize of Architectural Insititute of Japan, Japan

2007   Premio Mario Pani 2007 (The Mario Pani Award), Mexico

2007   The Kunstpreis Berlin (Berlin Art Prize), Germany

2010   The Pritzker Architecture Prize, USA

2011   Officer of the Order of Arts and Letters, France

2012   The Prize of Architectural Institute of Japan, Japan

2012   25th Murano Togo Prize

2013   The Silver T-square Prize, France

2014   Daylight Award, Switzerland

2016   Mies Crown Americas Prize, USA

Translation: Thomas Daniell (pp.8-9), Haruki Makio / Studio OJMM (pp.10-109)
Translation Assistance: Sam Chermayeff
Project Team: Ryue Nishizawa + Ippei Takahashi + Kenichi Fujisawa + Taeko Nakatsubo / Office of Ryue Nishizawa

現代建築家コンセプト・シリーズ 4

西沢立衛 西沢立衛建築設計事務所スタディ集

発 行 日　2009 年 4 月 15 日 第 1 刷発行
　　　　　2025 年 3 月　1 日 第 7 刷発行

著　　者　西沢立衛、髙橋一平

発 行 者　住友 千之

発 行 所　株式会社トゥーヴァージンズ
　　　　　〒 102-0073 東京都千代田区九段北 4-1-3
　　　　　TEL 03-5212-7442　FAX 03-5212-7889
　　　　　https://www.twovirgins.jp/

企画・編集　メディア・デザイン研究所

翻　　訳　トーマス・ダニエル、牧尾晴喜／株式会社フレーズクレーズ

装　　幀　町口覚

印　　刷　株式会社 山田写真製版所

　　　　　ISBN978-4-86791-043-6 C0052
　　　　　© 2009 by Office of Ryue Nishizawa, Printed in Japan

　　　　　乱丁・落丁本はお取替えいたします。
　　　　　本書の無断複写（コピー）は著作権法上での例外を除き、禁じられています。
　　　　　定価はカバーに表示しています。